Investment Management Regulation
Third Edition

Tamar Frankel

Professor of Law

Boston University School of Law

Clifford E. Kirsch

Chief Counsel, Variable Products

The Prudential Insurance Company of America

Adjunct Faculty, University of Pennsylvania Law School

And Benjamin N. Cardozo School of Law

Fathom Publishing Company

Anchorage, Alaska

To Ray and my children, Anat and Michael

—Tamar

For Teri – my best friend, girl friend and bride

—Cliff

ISBN 978-1-888215-07-6

Library of Congress Control Number: 2007933364

Fathom Publishing Company
P.O. Box 200448
Anchorage, Alaska 99520-0448
Telephone 907-272-3305
Fax 907-272-3305
E-mail publisher@teachmutualfunds.com
www.teachmutualfunds.com

Printed in the United States of America

Introduction

Much has happened in the area of investment management regulation during the past three years. Not only did the Commissioners at the Securities and Exchange Commission change more frequently than before, but also the whole area of pooled investments has been evolving. Hedge funds and private equity funds that have existed before grew in size to become an important force, shaping the financial scene. These funds are regulated differently and lightly as compared to investment companies. The SEC and private litigants' attempts to bring them under a stricter regulatory umbrella have not been fully successful to date. The materials below are important additions to the regulatory system, and include judicial reaction to the attempts of the SEC to expand its regulation over hedge funds, and the SEC's attempted adjustments to the new environment.

Tamar Frankel

Table of Contents

Table of Cases

Page 60. To the end of the page, add the following:

In recent years broker dealers began to charge asset-based fees or fixed fees rather than commissions. Such new fee measures would have eliminated the exception for broker dealers from the definition of an adviser and would have required them to register as such, even though the fees related only to their broker dealers services. Therefore, in April 12, 2005 the SEC adopted a rule that excluded broker dealers from the application of the Advisers Act notwithstanding their asset-based fees, under certain conditions.[*] The following is part of the summary of the rule as described by the SEC:

The Securities and Exchange Commission is adopting a rule addressing the application of the Investment Advisers Act of 1940 to broker-dealers offering certain types of brokerage programs. Under the rule, a broker-dealer providing advice that is solely incidental to its brokerage services is excepted from the Advisers Act if it charges an asset-based or fixed fee (rather than a commission, mark-up, or mark-down) for its services, provided it makes certain disclosures about the nature of its services. The rule states that exercising investment discretion is not "solely incidental to" the business of a broker or dealer within the meaning of the Advisers Act or to brokerage services within the meaning of the rule. The rule also states that a broker or dealer provides investment advice that is not solely incidental to the conduct of its business as a broker or dealer or to its brokerage services if the broker or dealer charges a separate fee or separately contracts for advisory services. In addition, the rule states that when a broker-dealer provides advice as part of a financial plan or in connection with providing planning services, a broker-dealer provides advice that is not solely incidental if it: holds itself out to the public as a financial planner or as providing financial planning services; or delivers to its customer a financial plan; or represents to the customer that the advice is provided as part of a financial plan or financial planning services. Finally, under the rule, broker-dealers are not subject to the Advisers Act solely because they offer full-service brokerage and discount brokerage services (including electronic brokerage) for reduced commission rates....

The SEC drew the following conclusion from the legislative history of the Advisers Act:

First, as drafted in 1940, the Advisers Act avoided additional and largely duplicative regulation of broker-dealers, which were regulated under provisions of the Exchange Act that had been enacted six years earlier. Second, the broker-dealer exception in the Advisers Act was understood to distinguish between broker-dealers who provided advice to customers only as part of the package of traditional brokerage services for which customers paid fixed commissions--who were not covered by the Advisers Act--and broker-dealers who also provided advisory services (typically through their special advisory departments) for which customers

---

[*] Certain Broker-Dealers Deemed Not To Be Investment Advisers, Investment Advisers Act Release No. 2376 (Apr. 12, 2005)

separately contracted and paid a fee--who were covered by the Act. As the legislative history shows, representatives of the investment counsel industry who participated in the Advisers Act hearings (and cooperated in drafting the version of the bill that Congress ultimately enacted) understood that broker-dealers offered investment advice both as part of their traditional commission brokerage services and, alternatively, for a separate fee through special departments, and that the Advisers Act was intended to reach only the latter. The earliest Commission staff interpretations of the Advisers Act also reflect the same understanding, *i.e.*, that the Act was intended to cover broker-dealers only to the extent that they were offering investment advice as a distinct service for which they were specifically compensated (which it was "well known" they were doing through special advisory departments).

Although, as discussed above, the Advisers Act was written in such a way that it covers fee-based programs because the fee would constitute "special compensation," we do not believe that it would be consistent with Congress' intent to apply the Act to cover broker-dealers providing advice as part of the package of brokerage services they provide under fee-based brokerage programs....

To the extent fee-based brokerage programs offer a package of the same types of services that Congress intended the Advisers Act *not* to cover, the rule we are adopting today is necessary to prevent the Act from reaching beyond Congress' intent. Today, fee-based brokerage programs are offered by most of the larger broker-dealers, and hold over $ 268 billion of customer assets. Although this is still a relatively small number, it is estimated that assets in fee-based brokerage programs nationwide grew by 60.9 percent during 2003-2004. Industry observers expect that fee-based programs will continue to grow as broker-dealers move away from transaction-based brokerage relationships that provide unsteady sources of revenue. Our failure to adopt this rule could eventually result in the extension of the Advisers Act to many brokerage relationships. Such a result would be inconsistent with the intent of the Advisers Act, which, as discussed earlier, was designed to fill a regulatory gap that had permitted firms and individuals to engage in advisory activities without being regulated. Moreover, such a result would create substantial regulatory overlap, which the Act was drafted to avoid. Far from being a radical departure from existing regulatory policy as suggested by some commenters, we believe the primary effect of rule 202(a)(11)-1 will be to maintain the historical ability of full-service broker-dealers to provide a wide variety of services, including advisory services, to brokerage customers, without requiring those broker-dealers to treat those clients as advisory clients.

*   *   *

After the passage of the rule the Financial Planning Association sued the SEC seeking a judicial decision that the SEC has exceeded its authority and striking down the rule. The D.C. Circuit agreed. Part of the decision is reproduced below.

Financial Planning Association v. SEC
482 F.3d 481 (D.C. Cir. 2007)*

* * * ROGERS, *Circuit Judge*: Brokers and dealers are not subject to the requirements of the Investment Advisers Act ("IAA") where their investment advice is (1) "solely incidental to the conduct of [their] business as a broker or dealer," and (2) the broker or dealer "receives no special compensation therefor." 15 U.S.C. § 80b-2(a)(11)(C) (2000). The Securities and Exchange Commission, acting pursuant to § 202(a)(11)(F) and § 211(a) of the IAA, 15 U.S.C. §§ 80b-2(a)(11)(F) [now (G)], 80b-11(a), promulgated a final rule exempting broker-dealers from the IAA when they receive "special compensation therefor." The Financial Planning Association ("FPA") petitions for review of the final rule on the ground that the SEC has exceeded its authority. We agree, and we therefore grant the petition and vacate the final rule.

I. *   *   *

Under the IAA [Investment Advisers Act], investment advisers are required, among other things, to register and to maintain records; to limit the type of contracts they enter; and not to engage in certain types of deceptive and fraudulent transactions. Congress has amended the IAA on several occasions, but the provisions at issue in this appeal have remained, in relevant part, unchanged.

In § 202(a)(11) of the IAA, Congress broadly defined "investment adviser" as

any person who, for compensation, engages in the business of advising others, either directly or through publications or writings, as to the value of securities or as to the advisability of investing in, purchasing, or selling securities, or who, for compensation and as part of a regular business, issues or promulgates analyses or reports concerning securities ...."

...Carving out six exemptions from this broad definition, Congress determined that an "investment adviser" did not include: ...

(C) any broker or dealer [1] whose performance of such services is solely incidental to the conduct of his business as a broker or dealer and [2] who receives no special compensation therefor...

(F) such other persons not within the intent of this paragraph, as the Commission may designate by rules and regulations or order. ...

Subsections (C) and (F) are at issue in this appeal.

Before enactment of the IAA, broker-dealers and others who offered investment advice received two general forms of compensation. Some charged only traditional commissions (earning a certain amount for each securities transaction completed). Others charged a separate advice fee (often a certain percentage of the customer's assets under advisement or supervision). The Committee Reports recognized that the statutory exemption for broker-dealers reflected this distinction; the Reports explained that the term "investment adviser" was "so defined as specifically to exclude ... brokers (insofar as their advice is merely incidental to brokerage transactions for which they receive only brokerage commissions)."

---

* Footnotes omitted. Some citations omitted.

The final rule took a different approach. After determining in 1999 that certain new forms of fee-contracting adopted by broker-dealers were "not ... fundamentally different from traditional brokerage programs," the SEC proposed a rule very similar to the final rule, stating it would act as if it had already issued the rule. In adopting the temporary rule, pursuant to subsection (F) and its general rulemaking authority under IAA § 211(a), the SEC exempted a new group of broker-dealers from the IAA. After re-proposing the rule in January 2005, again pursuant to its authority under subsection (F) and § 211(a), the SEC adopted a slightly modified final rule on April 12, 2005, codified at 17 C.F.R. § 275.202(a)(11)-1.

The final rule provides, generally, in Paragraph (a)(1), on "fee-based programs," that a broker-dealer who (1) receives special compensation will not be deemed an investment adviser if (2) any advice provided is solely incidental to brokerage services provided on a customer's account and (3) specific disclosure is made to the customer. In Paragraph (a)(2), on discount brokerage programs, a broker-dealer will not be deemed to have received special compensation merely because it charges one customer more or less for brokerage services than it charges another customer. Paragraph (b) lists three non-exclusive circumstances in which advisory services, for which special compensation is received under paragraph (a)(1), would not be performed "solely incidental to" brokerage: when (1) a separate fee or contract exists for advice; (2) a customer receives certain financial planning services; and, (3) generally, a broker-dealer has investment discretion over a client's account. Paragraph (c) states a "special rule" that broker-dealers registered under the Exchange Act are investment advisers only for those accounts for which they receive compensation that subjects them to the IAA. Paragraph (d) defines the term "investment discretion," which appears in paragraphs (a)(1) and (b)(3), to have the same meaning as § 3(a)(35) of the Exchange Act, 15 U.S.C. § 78c(a)(35), except for "discretion granted by a customer on a temporary or limited basis."

The FPA petitions for review, challenging the SEC's authority to promulgate the final rule. We first address the threshold issue presented by the SEC's challenge to FPA's standing.

II.

[The Court found that the FPA had standing to bring its petition.]

III.

The FPA contends that when Congress enacted the IAA, Congress identified in subsection (C) the group of broker-dealers it intended to exempt, and that subsection (F) was only intended to allow the SEC to exempt new groups from the IAA, not to expand the groups that Congress specifically addressed. The resolution of the FPA's challenge thus turns on whether the SEC is authorized under § 202(a)(11)(F) or § 211(a) to except from IAA coverage an additional group of broker-dealers beyond the broker-dealers exempted by Congress in subsection (C), 15 U.S.C. § 80b-2(a)(11)(C). Subsection (F) of § 202(a)(11) authorizes the SEC to except from the IAA "such other persons not within the intent of this paragraph, as the Commission may designate by rules and regulations or order." 15 U.S.C. § 80b-2(a)(11)(F). As such, we review the SEC's exercise of its authority pursuant to subsection (F) under the familiar two-step analysis of *Chevron, USA, Inc. v. Natural Res. Def. Counsel, Inc.* Under step one, the court must determine whether Congress has directly spoken to the precise question at issue. "If the intent of Congress is clear, that is the end of the matter; for the court, as well as the agency, must give effect to the unambiguously expressed intent of Congress." Under step two, "if the statute is silent or ambiguous with respect to the specific issue, the question for the court is whether the agency's answer is based on a permissible construction of the statute." In reviewing an agency's interpretation of its authority under a statute it administers, the court will uphold that interpretation as long as it is a reasonable interpretation of the statute.

Applying the "traditional tools of statutory construction," the court looks to the text, structure, and the overall statutory scheme, as well as the problem Congress sought to solve. All four elements demonstrate that the SEC has exceeded its authority in promulgating the rule under § 202(a)(11)(F) because Congress has addressed the precise issue at hand.

Section 202(a)(11) lists exemptions (A)-(E) from the broad definition of "investment adviser" for several classes of persons -- including, for example, lawyers, accountants, and others whose advice is "solely incidental" to their regular business; and publishers of newsletters that circulate widely and do not give individually-tailored financial advice. Among the IAA exemptions is subsection (C)'s exemption for "*any* broker or dealer whose performance of such [investment advisory] services is solely incidental to the conduct of his business as a broker or dealer and who receives no special compensation therefor." (Emphasis added). Beyond the listed exemptions, subsection (F) authorizes the SEC to exempt from the IAA "such *other* persons not within the intent of this paragraph, as the Commission may designate by rules and regulations or order." (Emphasis added).

In the final rule, the SEC purports to use its authority under subsection (F) to broaden the exemption for broker-dealers provided under subsection (C). The rule is inconsistent with the IAA, however, because it fails to meet either of the two requirements for an exemption under subsection (F). First, the legislative "intent" does not support an exemption for broker-dealers broader than the exemption set forth in the text of subsection (C); therefore, the final rule does not meet the statutory requirement that exemptions under subsection (F) be consistent with the "intent" of paragraph 11 of section 202(a). Second, because broker-dealers are already expressly addressed in subsection (C), they are not "other persons" under subsection (F); therefore the SEC cannot use its authority under subsection (F) to establish new, broader exemptions for broker-dealers.

The final rule's exemption for broker-dealers is broader than the statutory exemption for broker-dealers under subsection (C). Although the SEC maintains that the intent of paragraph 11 is to exempt broker-dealers who receive special compensation for investment advice, the plain text of subsection (C) exempts only broker-dealers who do not receive special compensation for investment advice. The word "any" is usually understood to be all inclusive. As "[t]he plain meaning of legislation should be conclusive, except in the 'rare cases [in which] the literal application of a statute will produce a result demonstrably at odds with the intentions of its drafters,'" the terms of the IAA establish the precise conditions under which broker-dealers are exempt from the IAA. "To read out of a statutory provision a clause setting forth a specific condition or trigger to the provision's applicability is ... an entirely unacceptable method of construing statutes."

No other indicators of congressional intent support the SEC's interpretation of its authority under subsection (F). The relevant language in the committee reports suggests that Congress deliberately drafted the exemption in subsection (C) to apply as written. Those reports stated that the "term 'investment adviser' is so defined as specifically to exclude ... brokers (insofar as their advice is merely incidental to brokerage transactions for which they receive *only* brokerage commissions)." By seeking to exempt broker-dealers beyond those who receive only brokerage commissions for investment advice, the SEC has promulgated a final rule that is in direct conflict with both the statutory text and the Committee Reports.

The text of subsection (F) confirms this conclusion by the limiting the SEC's exemption authorization to "other persons." We agree with the FPA that when Congress enacted the IAA, Congress identified the specific classes of persons it intended to exempt. As to broker-dealers, subsection (C) applied to "*any* broker or dealer." Congress, through the use of contrasting text in subsection (F), signaled that it only authorized the SEC to exempt " *other* persons" when consistent with the intent of the paragraph, and thus only when doing so would not override Congress's determination of the appropriate persons to be exempted from the IAA's requirements.

As the FPA points out, the word "other" connotes "existing besides, or distinct from, that already mentioned or implied." There is nothing to suggest that Congress did not intend the words "any" or "other" to have their "ordinary or natural meaning." So understood, courts have hesitated to allow parties to use language structurally similar to the "other persons" clause in subsection (F) to redefine or otherwise avoid specific requirements in existing statutory exceptions. In *Liljeberg v. Health Servs. Acquisition Corp.*, for example, the Supreme Court noted that where Federal Rule of Civil Procedure 60(b) contained five explicit grounds for relief, and one non-specific "any *other* reason" clause, (emphasis added) the structure of the clauses suggested that the final clause could not be used to elude or enlarge the first five -- that "clause (6) and clauses (1) through (5) are *mutually exclusive*." (emphasis added). Similarly, in *Am. Bankers Ass'n v. SEC*, this court explained that:

> A universal clause preceding every definition in the statute, which states only "unless the context otherwise requires," cannot provide the authority for one of the agencies whose jurisdictional boundaries are defined in the statute to alter by administrative regulation those very jurisdictional boundaries. To suggest otherwise is to sanction administrative autonomy beyond the control of either Congress or the courts.

Our dissenting colleague attempts to distinguish these two cases as limited to situations in which one agency seeks to redraw the jurisdictional boundaries of another agency. That interpretation, however, ignores the underlying principle in each case: where the statutory text is clear, an agency may not use general clauses to redefine the jurisdictional boundaries set by the statute.

Just as the text and structure of paragraph of 202(a)(11) make it evident that Congress intended to define "investment adviser" broadly and create only a precise exemption for broker-dealers, so does a consideration of the problems Congress sought to address in enacting the IAA. A comprehensive study conducted by the SEC pursuant to the Public Utility Holding Company Act of 1935 indicated that "many investment counsel have 'strayed a great distance from that professed function' of furnishing disinterested, personalized, continuous supervision of investments." Floor debate on the IAA called attention to the fact that while this study was being conducted investment trusts and investment companies had perpetrated "some of the most flagrant abuses and grossest violations of fiduciary duty to investors." Congress reiterated throughout its proceedings an intention to protect investors and bona fide investment advisers.

The overall statutory scheme of the IAA addresses the problems identified to Congress in two principal ways: First, by establishing a federal fiduciary standard to govern the conduct of investment advisers, broadly defined, and second, by requiring full disclosure of all conflicts of interest. As the Supreme Court noted, Congress's "broad proscription against 'any ... practice ... which operates ... as a fraud or deceit upon any client or prospective client' remained in the bill from beginning to end."

> [T]he Committee Reports indicate a desire to ... eliminate conflicts of interest between the investment adviser and the clients as safeguards both to 'unsophisticated investors' and to 'bona fide investment counsel.' The [IAA] thus reflects a ... congressional intent to eliminate, or at least to expose, all conflicts of interest which might incline an investment adviser -- consciously or unconsciously -- to render advice which was not disinterested.

This statutory scheme is inconsistent with a construction of the SEC's authority under subsection (F) that would enable persons Congress determined should be subject to the IAA to escape its restrictions.

In an attempt to overcome the plain language of the statute, the SEC asserts that Congress was also concerned about the regulation of broker-dealers under both the IAA and Exchange Act, and that such concern was reflected in the "intent" of the paragraph. The SEC points to no convincing evidence that supports these assertions. At the time Congress enacted the IAA in 1940, broker-dealers were already regulated under the Exchange Act. In the IAA, Congress expressly acknowledged that the broker-dealers it covered could also be subject to other regulation. IAA § 208(b), 15 U.S.C. § 80b-8(b). The IAA's essential purpose was to "protect the public from the frauds and misrepresentations of unscrupulous tipsters and touts and to safeguard the honest investment adviser against the stigma of the activities of these individuals by making fraudulent practices by investment advisers unlawful." As the FPA emphasizes, there is nothing in the committee reports to suggest that Congress was particularly concerned about the regulatory burdens on broker-dealers.

While the SEC's failure to respect the unambiguous textual limitations marked by the phrase "intent of this paragraph" and "other persons" is fatal to the final rule, an additional weakness exists in the SEC's interpretation: It flouts six decades of consistent SEC understanding of its authority under subsection (F). Subsection (F) is not a catch-all that authorizes the SEC to rewrite the statute. Rather, as subsection (F)'s terms provide, the authority conferred must be exercised consistent with the "intent of this paragraph" and apply to "other persons." The SEC cannot point to any instance between the 1940 enactment of the IAA and the commencement of the rulemaking proceedings that resulted in the final rule in 2005, when it attempted to invoke subsection (F) to alter or rewrite the exemptions for persons qualifying for exemptions under subsections (A)-(E). Rather, the SEC has historically invoked subsection (F) to exempt persons not otherwise addressed in the five exemptions established by Congress: For example, the adviser to a family trust who was otherwise subject to fiduciary duties; or new groups, such as thrift institutions acting in a fiduciary capacity, and World Bank instrumentalities that provide advice only to sovereigns. As the SEC's own actions for the last 65 years suggest, subsection (F) serves the clear purpose of authorizing the SEC to address persons or classes involving situations that Congress had not foreseen in the statutory text -- not to broaden the exemptions of the classes of persons (such as broker-dealers) Congress had expressly addressed.

The SEC unconvincingly attempts to defend its expansive interpretation of subsection (F) by likening it to section 6(c) of the ICA, 15 U.S.C. § 80a-6(c). Section 6(c) of the ICA empowers the SEC to grant exemptions from the ICA, or any rule or regulation adopted under it, "if and to the extent that such exemption is necessary or appropriate in the public interest and consistent with the protection of investors and the purposes fairly intended by the policy and provisions" of the ICA. This court has noted that the SEC "has exercised this authority to exempt persons not within the intent of the [ICA] and generally to adjust its provisions to take account of special situations not foreseen when the [ICA] was drafted." Reliance on *NASD* does not advance the SEC's position as the plain text of the ICA is far broader than that of IAA subsection (F). The ICA expressly refers to the SEC's view of "the public interest" as a basis for new exemptions. "[W]e assume that in drafting ... legislation, Congress said what it meant." Although Congress amended the IAA in 1970, and repeated the same ICA language highlighted in *NASD* in § 206A of the IAA, 15 U.S.C. § 80b-6a, the SEC disavows any reliance on § 206A in promulgating the final rule, and thus the court has no occasion to express an opinion on the SEC's authority under it. But the broader language found in § 206A supports the conclusion that subsection (F) must be read more narrowly.

In light of the context in which Congress drafted subsections (C) and (F), we conclude that, as indicated by the structure of § 202(a)(11) and the problems that Congress addressed in the IAA, as well as the other indicators of Congress's intent, under *Chevron* step one the text of subsections (C) and (F) is unambiguous, and that, therefore, the SEC has exceeded its authority in promulgating the final rule.... Because the court's duty is to give meaning to each word of a statute, the court cannot properly treat one authorization, under subsection (F), as duplicative of another authorization, under Section 206A. Consequently, section 202(a)(11)(F) does not lend itself to alternative meanings; to conclude otherwise would undermine Congress's purpose in enacting the IAA-to protect consumers and honest investment advisers and to establish fiduciary standards and require full disclosure of all conflicts of interests of "investment advisers," broadly defined. The SEC's suggestion that "new" broker-dealer marketing developments fall within the scope of its authority under subsection (F) ignores its own contemporaneous understanding of Congressional intent to capture such developments. Although an agency may change its interpretation of an ambiguous statute, all elements of the traditional tools of statutory interpretation confound the SEC's effort to walk away from its long-settled view of the limits of its authority under subsection (F) and our dissenting colleague's attempt to find an alternative meaning at this late date.

The SEC's invocation of its general rulemaking authority under IAA section 211(a), is likewise to no avail because it suggests no intention by Congress that the SEC could ignore either of the two requirements in subsection (C) for broker-dealers to be exempt from the IAA. Paraphrasing an apt observation, while, in the SEC's view, "[t]he statute may be imperfect, ... the [SEC] has no power to correct flaws that it perceives in the statute it is empowered to administer. Its [subsection (F) authority and its] rulemaking power[s] [are] limited to adopting regulations to carry into effect the will of Congress as expressed in the statute."

Accordingly, we grant the petition and vacate the final rule.... [Dissent omitted].

Page 104. After the Discussion Topics, insert the following:

SEC v. National Presto Industries, Inc.

486 F.3d 305 (7th Cir. 2007)[*]

EASTERBROOK, *Chief Judge*. Most mutual funds and other investment companies come within the scope of the Investment Company Act of 1940 because they hold themselves out "as being engaged primarily, or propos[ing] to engage primarily, in the business of investing, reinvesting, or trading in securities". 15 U.S.C. § 80a-3(a)(1)(A). But firms can be dragged within the Act's coverage kicking and screaming, even though they depict themselves as operating businesses rather than as managing other people's money. Any issuer that owns "investment securities" worth 40% of its total assets is an investment company under § 80a-3(a)(1)(C) unless some other provision of the Act takes it outside the definition. For this purpose, however, "Government securities and cash items" are omitted from both the numerator and the denominator.

National Presto Industries, a seller of both consumer goods (cookware, diapers, and other household items) and munitions, used to make everything it sold. During the 1970s it began to divest its manufacturing facilities and to contract production to third parties. In 1993 the Department of Defense closed a facility that Presto had used to make artillery shells. Presto was left with a pile of cash, most of which it retained with a long-term plan to acquire other businesses, and a shrunken book value of operating assets. Financial instruments were 86% of its total assets by 1994 and 92% in 1998. Since 2000 Presto has purchased two manufacturers of military supplies and two makers of diapers and puppy pads. But in 2003 financial instruments still represented 62% of its physical and financial assets. Intellectual property, although of considerable value to Presto, is not carried on corporate books at its full economic value, so this ratio overstates the significance of its portfolio of securities, but Presto does not argue that it could come under the 40% ratio by marking its patents and trademarks to current market value.

All of Presto's consumer products other than absorbent products are made by subcontractors, so although it has a substantial operating *income* it does not have operating *assets* to match--and the Investment Company Act's main test is asset-based. The SEC concluded that Presto was well past the 40% trigger. When the firm refused to register as an investment company--and make the changes to its corporate structure, management, and financial reporting required of investment companies--or request an administrative exemption, the SEC filed this suit to seek an injunction that would require compliance. After preliminary maneuvering vindicated the SEC's choice of forum, see 347 F.3d 662 (7th Cir. 2003), the district court granted summary judgment in the agency's favor, 397 F. Supp. 2d 943 (N.D. Ill. 2005), and issued an injunction requiring Presto to register under the 1940 Act. The firm has complied pending appeal.

---

[*] Some citations omitted.

After suffering defeat on the merits, Presto replaced enough of its existing portfolio with "Government securities and cash items" to bring investment securities under the 40% threshold. The SEC had proposed an injunction that would have allowed Presto the opportunity to do this (or to seek an administrative exemption) in lieu of registration; the firm thought to avail itself of the opportunity even before the injunction was entered.

Without inviting comment from the parties, however, the district judge deleted these options from the SEC's draft and entered an injunction unconditionally requiring Presto to register as an investment company. The judge did not explain why. The result was a regulatory mismatch: a firm that is today required (by statute) to be organized and to report its financial position as an operating company is required (by injunction) to be organized and report its financial position as an investment company. Instead of doing this, the district court would have been well advised to craft an injunction commanding registration only if Presto should revert to its old portfolio design; obliging it to register as an investment company even when its investments do not require this is hard to fathom except as a form of punishment for Presto's conduct in past years, and civil injunctions are not supposed to punish litigants.

The unconditional injunction has caused considerable trouble. Investment companies are subject to many governance requirements that do not apply to operating companies.... Presto's auditor, Grant Thornton, resigned because the SEC questioned its certification of Presto's financial statements as those of an operating company. Now that Presto is officially an investment company, Grant Thornton has refused to allow the statements it certified to be used for any purpose. This has disabled Presto from complying fully with *either* the Investment Company Act or the Securities Exchange Act of 1934. Without the financial statements, it is unable to file quarterly and annual reports. It has hired another auditor, but recreating and re-certifying financial statements for many past years is expensive and time consuming. Meanwhile stock exchanges have threatened to delist its stock because Presto is out of compliance with both statutory and exchange-based financial-reporting requirements.

At oral argument we inquired whether Presto's financial rearrangement has made the case moot. Now that it has complied with the injunction by registering as an investment company, can't it deregister and go back to its preferred status as an operating company, subject to registration under the Securities Exchange Act, no matter what happens on appeal? Deregistration requires the consent of the SEC, however, and although Presto filed the appropriate papers with the agency in January 2006 the SEC has failed to act on them.

One senses from this prolonged silence, and the tenor of the SEC's brief and oral argument, that the agency (or its senior staff) is in a snit because Presto declined to do what many other firms with excess liquid assets have done--apply to the agency for an exemption. See 15 U.S.C. § 80a-3(b)(2). (Microsoft, for example, holds more than 40% of its assets in the form of investment securities but received permission to operate outside the 1940 Act.) The agency's counsel implied at oral argument that an exemption would have been forthcoming if sought. Yet a firm's refusal to kowtow to an agency is not a good reason to force its investors to bear unnecessary costs--for it is the investors who must pay to recreate the financial statements, though *they* did not contribute to this imbroglio--and keep a firm inappropriately registered, as Presto now is. Why is the SEC bent on grinding down a corporation that it appears to acknowledge would not mislead or otherwise injure investors by using the governance and reporting devices appropriate to an operating company?

Because Presto remains registered as an investment company while the SEC sits on its hands, there is a live case or controversy, because a remedy is possible: we could end its registration forthwith. Moreover, if we hold that Presto's former portfolio does not bring it within the Investment Company Act, it will be free to rejigger its investments; the old investments likely had a higher rate of return, which is why Presto switched only after the district court's opinion.

Let us begin, then, with Presto's argument that even before the recent changes to its portfolio, enough of its investments were "Government securities and cash items" to keep its "investment securities" under the 40% trigger.

"Government securities" is a defined term. The phrase "means any security issued or guaranteed as to principal or interest by the United States, or by a person controlled or supervised by and acting as an instrumentality of the Government of the United States pursuant to authority granted by the Congress of the United States; or any certificate of deposit for any of the foregoing." 15 U.S.C. § 80a-2(a)(16). According to Presto, pre-refunded municipal bonds ("refunded bonds" for short) fit this definition. Presto held these instruments in quantity.

A refunded bond is a bond backed by U.S. securities as well as the credit of the issuer. Suppose that a municipality issues long-term bonds for a project (say, an airport) and that the market rate of interest later falls. The issuer would like to take advantage of the lower rate, but the bonds lack a call feature. The municipality can issue new bonds at the current lower rate and use the proceeds to buy Treasury bonds with the same maturity as the original issue of municipal bonds. The Treasury securities are held in trust to pay interest and principal on the original issue. The municipality pays the interest on the new issue; the Treasury securities may cover the old issue, and if not the municipality can chip in the difference. Refinancing in this way works because municipal bonds are not subject to federal taxes, so they often pay lower interest rates than Treasury securities. Bonds that can be bought with the proceeds of the new municipal issue may produce enough interest by themselves to cover the interest on the old issue.

The Treasury bonds held in trust lead Presto to call the refunded bonds themselves "Government securities." It should be apparent, however, that they do not fit the statutory definition. Refunded municipal bonds are still municipal bonds, exactly as they were before the refunding transaction. Municipal bonds are neither issued nor guaranteed by the national government or any federal instrumentality. If the municipality defaults, or a local employee reaches into the till and makes off with the Treasury securities, the national government will not cover the loss. The bonds in trust make the municipal bonds safer, but 15 U.S.C. § 80a-2(a)(16) does not include in the category of "Government securities" everything that a company deems "almost as safe as" Treasury securities.

The argument "X has the same economic attributes as Y, so X must have the same legal attributes as Y" has a history in securities law. It was the basis of the sale-of-business doctrine that many courts accepted before *Landreth Timber Co. v. Landreth.* The idea was that someone who bought all of the stock in a closely-held corporation was buying the corporation's assets, as an economic matter, so the transaction should not be governed by the securities laws. *Landreth Timber* held, however, that someone who wants the legal treatment of an asset acquisition must buy the assets rather than the stock; people may choose between transacting in securities and transacting in assets, and the law follows the form--not only because that is what the statute says, but also because trying to determine, one case at a time, when a transaction "really" has the economic attributes of a different form would lead to a great deal of uncertainty for little purpose. *Landreth Timber* represents the norm in securities law. Stock or bonds in a company that invests the proceeds in land, or gold, or art, are still regulated as securities rather than as land, or gold, or art. Pooled interests in orange groves are regulated as investment contracts rather than as oranges. And municipal bonds issued by a city that plans to repay using U.S. bonds are still municipal bonds.

Securities laws regulate the form of financial transactions, rather than looking through form to substance. True enough, § 80a-2 begins, as several other definitional clauses in the securities laws do, with the phrase, "unless the context otherwise requires." ... We know ... from *Landreth Timber*, that this use of the context clause cannot be generalized into a norm that substance trumps form....But nothing in § 80a-3(a)(1)(C) similarly "requires" a departure from the definition in § 80a-2(a)(16). The definition of the phrase "Government securities" in the latter makes perfect sense when plugged into the former.

Judge Friendly once remarked, with respect to the definition of the term "note" in the securities laws: "So long as the statutes remain as they have been for over forty years, courts had better not depart from their words without strong support for the conviction that, under the authority vested in them by the 'context' clause, they are doing what Congress wanted when they refuse to do what it said. " That high standard has not been met here. The Investment Company Act has been with us for 67 years without giving problems through the definition of "Government securities." And even if there were some wriggle room via the context clause, Presto has not established that refunded bonds are the economic equivalent of Treasury bonds. A report in the record from Morgan Stanley shows that the yield for Treasury bonds maturing in 2006 was 4.95%, while the taxable equivalent yield for refunded bonds was 6.1% for taxpayers in the 38% bracket. That's a 23% premium over Treasuries, which must reflect extra risk. (The nominal interest rate for refunded bonds is below that for Treasury bonds, because of the tax subsidy for municipal securities; an adjustment must be made to find real returns and implicit risks.)

Mutual funds may treat refunded bonds as if they were "Government securities" for the purpose of 15 U.S.C. § 80a-5, which says how an investment company's portfolio must be structured if it calls itself "diversified." See 17 C.F.R. § 270.5b-3(b). How can refunded bonds be "Government securities" for one purpose but not the other?, Presto asks. Yet treating A as if it were B for one purpose does not imply that A *is* B for every purpose. The regulation on which Presto relies governs how investment companies describe their portfolios; that's a very different subject from whether something is an investment company in the first place. Equating refunded bonds with Treasury securities for the purpose of diversification allows mutual funds to offer tax advantages (which refunded bonds supply) without any change in the covariance of risk across a fund's assets. Denying investors that opportunity would injure them; it's sensible for the SEC to look at the economic attributes of instruments when determining what counts as diversification (another economic inquiry) while insisting that the statutory definition be used to determine what entities are covered by the statute in the first place.

"Cash items" also are excluded when calculating the 40% ratio, and Presto maintains that "variable-rate demand notes" should be treated as "cash items." A variable-rate demand note is an instrument (usually a bond or debenture) whose rate of interest is updated weekly (if not more often) based on some index, such as the London Interbank Offering Rate. Whenever the interest rate changes, the note's holder is entitled to redeem at par. Usually this transaction is handled by a remarketing agent, who buys the note from the holder and resells it in the secondary market to another investor; the note's issuer is involved only if the note is trading for less than par.

In contrast to the detailed statutory definition of "Government securities," the Investment Company Act does not define "cash items." Presto maintains that variable-rate demand notes are equivalent to cash because of the weekly opportunity to sell the instruments at par for cash. If liquidity were enough, however, one would treat all shares of stock in large issuers, and many bonds, as "cash items" because they can be sold on liquid markets in a matter of minutes. The reason that such investments are not treated as cash or its equivalent, however, is that the market price the instrument will fetch when sold is variable. Presto thinks that the "redeem at par" feature of the variable-rate demand note insulates them from that sort of risk, but that's not true. The investor is entitled to *demand* redemption at par, but whether the issuer will comply depends on its financial health. A business reverse (or, for a municipal issuer, a shortfall of taxes) will mean no redemption, or redemption at a discount. That's a kind of risk an investor takes with any stock or bond--but does not take with cash.

Although the statute does not define "cash item," the SEC gave this definition when adopting a safe-harbor rule (17 C.F.R. § 270.3a-1):

> For purposes of determining compliance with the proposed rule, cash, coins, paper currency, demand deposits with banks, timely checks of others (which are orders on banks to immediately supply funds), cashier checks, certified checks, bank drafts, money orders, traveler's checks and letters of credit generally would be considered cash items. Certificates of deposit and time deposits typically would not be considered cash items absent convincing evidence of no investment intent.

This definition applies only to Rule 3a-1, but Presto does not contend that we should ignore it--or that it is arbitrary or capricious. Agencies are entitled to add detail to the statutes they administer, and their resolution of ambiguities is entitled to respect.

A variable-rate demand note does not fit this definition. Presto chose to invest in variable-rate demand notes rather than, say, money-market funds (which are diversified portfolios of safe and liquid investments) because the notes have higher rates of return. The higher return stems from higher risk, which explains why the notes differ from "cash items." (Presto does observe that many variable-rate demand notes are backed by letters of credit, which the SEC is willing to treat as "cash items," but that's a replay of the argument that refunded bonds are "Government securities" because they are secured by Treasury bonds.) Presto was making an *investment* in these notes, along the lines of "time deposits" (which are "cash items" only with "convincing evidence of no investment intent"), rather than holding them for liquidity.

Presto therefore comes within the 40% test and is an investment company unless one of the (many) statutory exceptions applies. The one on which Presto relies is § 80a-3(b)(1): "Any issuer primarily engaged, directly or through a wholly-owned subsidiary or subsidiaries, in a business or businesses other than that of investing, reinvesting, owning, holding, or trading in securities." Presto is actively engaged in several businesses. A visitor to its web site for consumers will find sales promotions, warranty information, and instruction manuals for pizza ovens and coffee makers but nary a hint that someone would want to buy Presto's stock as a means to own a derivative interest in refunded municipal bonds or variable-rate demand notes. But is Presto "primarily" engaged in selling pressure cookers, deep fryers, popcorn poppers, diapers, and ordnance rather than the business of holding securities? The statute is unhelpful; "primarily" is not a defined term. No regulation fills the gap.

Sixty years ago the SEC announced that it would consider five factors to decide whether a firm that sold off its operating assets and chose not to distribute the proceeds to its stockholders had become what people today call an "inadvertent investment company ." *In re Tonopah Mining Co.* (1959).

According to *Tonopah*, what matter are the company's history, the way the company represents itself to the investing public today, the activities of its officers and directors, the nature of its assets, and the sources of its income. Of these, all but the fourth favor Presto. Founded in 1905, Presto was an active manufacturer of industrial, consumer, and military products until the 1980s, when it started to subcontract manufacturing activities. It remains an active manufacturer of absorbent goods and military ordnance and sells a line of kitchen goods under its own trademarks.

As far as we can see, this is the first time that the SEC has argued that a firm with such a substantial ongoing presence in product markets is an inadvertent investment company. The model inadvertent investment company--of which Tonopah Mining is the initial exemplar and Fifth Avenue Coach Lines is perhaps the best-known,--is one in which the firm has sold all or almost all of its assets, reduced its operations to a skeleton staff (Tonopah Mining was down to one unprofitable mine and Fifth Avenue Coach Lines to no busses at all), and purports to be looking for acquisitions but never seems to find them. Perhaps one could have applied the "purports to be looking for acquisitions" label to Presto in the 1980s and 1990s, but one could *not* say that Presto had withdrawn from active business operations in the meantime. It continued selling both consumer and military products. It changed from a manufacturer to a firm that was (principally) a designer and marketer of products assembled by others, but this did not make Presto less an operating enterprise. Many other firms have made a similar transition (Apple comes to mind) without being thought to have evolved into mutual funds.

Presto presents itself to the public (and to investors) as an operating company. That's how its web site, its annual reports, and its publicity all depict it. The contrast with Tonopah Mining and Fifth Avenue Coach Lines is stark. An investor in the market for a mutual fund, a hedge fund, or any other investment pool would not dream of turning to Presto, whose net income can increase or decrease substantially as a result of business successes or reverses. The price of Presto's stock moves in response to changes in its operating profits rather than the slight annual changes in its investment income. The SEC has not identified even one confused investor who bought stock in Presto thinking that he was making an investment in a closed-end mutual fund whose assets were the securities that Presto holds.

"Activities of Officers and Directors," the third factor in *Tonopah*, likewise favors Presto. Directors and senior managers at Tonopah Mining and Fifth Avenue Coach Lines spent most of their time managing the firms' investment portfolios. Presto estimates that 95% of its managers' time is devoted to running its consumer-products and military-ordnance businesses. The SEC has not offered any contrary evidence.

As for the fifth factor, income, *Tonopah* looked at both gross and net figures, as well as at the firm's expenditures to produce income. (Looking at both gross and net is essential; otherwise an operating loss, with negative net income, would turn a firm into an "investment company".) Gross income at Presto is dominated by receipts from its consumer and military sales. More than 90% of Presto's gross receipts for every year covered by the record (1994 through 2003) comes from its sales of products. In 2003, for example, Presto recorded about $ 125 million in sales, yielding a net profit of $ 18.9 million; total receipts from investment securities that year were $ 4.2 million.

Only net income helps the SEC's position: the agency calculates that, over the decade covered by the record, 50.22% of Presto's net profits were derived from investments in securities. Presto's calculations show that operating profits exceed investment profits for the decade as a whole. The SEC acknowledges that, in each of the three years immediately preceding the district court's injunction requiring Presto to register as an investment company, investments produced less than 40% of Presto's net profit. So even if we take the view most favorable to the SEC, that a firm is "primarily" engaged in a business other than investment management only if more than half of its net profits come from non-investment sources, Presto was "primarily" an operating business when the injunction issued. Whatever classification may have been appropriate in the 1990s (when more than half of net profits came from investments) cannot support an injunction issued in 2005, when at least 60% of net profit was coming from consumer and military sales. In *Tonopah*, by contrast, "the company's only source of net income consists of interest, dividends and profits on the sale of securities; and we find nothing to indicate that this situation will be changed substantially in the foreseeable future."

This leaves the fourth *Tonopah* factor, the nature of Presto's assets. Here the picture at last favors the SEC, for more than 60% of Presto's assets were investment securities during every year covered by the record. In full flight from the Commission's multi-factor approach in *Tonopah*, the SEC's lawyer in this court urges us to give little weight to any consideration other than Presto's asset structure. Yet looking primarily at accounting assets has a potential to mislead. Imagine a firm that owns substantial assets such as patents and trademarks that do not show up on its balance sheet as assets, and that operates a business from a leased headquarters where it designs, contracts for, and sells products. Such a firm could have annual sales exceeding $ 100 million, and profits exceeding $ 10 million as Presto does, with book-value assets of only $ 1 million in office furniture. If that firm stored even 10% of two years' profits in refunded bonds, as a hedge against business reverses (or to finance expansion), instead of distributing all profits to investors in dividends, it would become an investment company under the approach the SEC urges in this litigation. Yet no investor would perceive such a firm as a substitute for a closed-end mutual fund; its stock returns would continue to depend on its operating profits and losses.

According to the SEC's brief, *Tonopah* deemed assets the "most important" of the five considerations. It would be surprising if that were so, because it would make the exclusion in § 80a-3(b)(1) unavailable as a practical matter. The only reason one turns to this exclusion is that the 40% asset test has been satisfied. If subsection (b)(2) does nothing except raise the 40% test to 50% as a definition of the firm's "primary" engagement, it is an odd statutory provision indeed. What sense would it make to enact a law using 40% as the threshold in subsection (a)(1)(C), and convert the "real" rule to 50% in subsection (b)(1) by using words rather than numbers? Subsection (b)(1) has to be about considerations other than assets (or at least in addition to assets). And that's what the SEC said in *Tonopah*:

> More important . . . [is] the nature of the assets and income of the company, disclosed in the annual reports filed with the Commission and in reports sent to stockholders, was such as *to lead investors to believe* that the principal *activity* of the company was trading and investing in securities.

In other words, the Commission thought in *Tonopah* that what principally matters is the beliefs the company is likely to induce in investors. Will its portfolio and activities lead investors to treat a firm as an investment vehicle or as an operating enterprise? The Commission has never issued an opinion or rule taking a different view, and its lawyers cannot adopt a new approach by filing briefs. Only the Commission's members may change established norms, and they must do so by rulemaking or administrative adjudication.

Reasonable investors would treat Presto as an operating company rather than a competitor with a closed-end mutual fund. The SEC has not tried to demonstrate anything different about investors' perceptions or behavior. It follows that Presto is not an investment company.

The judgment of the district court is reversed. Presto, which registered as an investment company only under judicial compulsion, now is free to drop that registration and operate under the Securities Exchange Act of 1934 whether or not the SEC gives its formal approach to that step.

*　　*　　*

Pages 139-40. Substitute, for the paragraph "In December 2004" and the following block quotation, the following:

Goldstein v. SEC
451 F.3d 873 (D.C. Cir. 2006)*

RANDOLPH, *Circuit Judge*: This is a petition for review of the Securities and Exchange Commission's regulation of "hedge funds" under the Investment Advisers Act of 1940, 15 U.S.C. § 80b-1 *et seq. See* Registration Under the Advisers Act of Certain Hedge Fund Advisers, 69 Fed. Reg. 72,054 (Dec. 10, 2004) (codified at 17 C.F.R. pts. 275, 279) ("*Hedge Fund Rule*"). Previously exempt because they had "fewer than fifteen clients," 15 U.S.C. § 80b-3(b)(3) , most advisers to hedge funds must now register with the Commission if the funds they advise have fifteen or more "shareholders, limited partners, members, or beneficiaries." 17 C.F.R. § 275.203(b)(3)-2(a). Petitioners Philip Goldstein, an investment advisory firm Goldstein co-owns (Kimball & Winthrop), and Opportunity Partners L.P., a hedge fund in which Kimball & Winthrop is the general partner and investment adviser (collectively "Goldstein") challenge the regulation's equation of "client" with "investor."

I.

"Hedge funds" are notoriously difficult to define. The term appears nowhere in the federal securities laws, and even industry participants do not agree upon a single definition. The term is commonly used as a catch-all for "any pooled investment vehicle that is privately organized, administered by professional investment managers, and not widely available to the public."

Hedge funds may be defined more precisely by reference to what they are *not*. The Investment Company Act of 1940, 15 U.S.C. § 80a-1 *et seq.*, directs the Commission to regulate any issuer of securities that "is or holds itself out as being engaged primarily . . . in the business of investing, reinvesting, or trading in securities." *Id.* § 80a-3(a)(1)(A). Although this definition nominally describes hedge funds, most are exempt from the Investment Company Act's coverage because they have one hundred or fewer beneficial owners and do not offer their securities to the public, *id.* § 80a-3(c)(1), or because their investors are all "qualified" high net-worth individuals or institutions, *id.* § 80a-3(c)(7). Investment vehicles that remain private and available only to highly sophisticated investors have historically been understood not to present the same dangers to public markets as more widely available investment companies, like mutual funds. Hedge funds are usually differentiated from other exempted investment vehicles like private equity or venture capital funds by their investing and governance behavior.

Exemption from regulation under the Investment Company Act allows hedge funds to engage in very different investing behavior than their mutual fund counterparts. While mutual funds, for example, must register with the Commission and disclose their investment positions and financial condition, *id.* §§ 80a-8, 80a-29, hedge funds typically remain secretive about their positions and strategies, even to

---

* Footnotes omitted. Some citations omitted.

their own investors. The Investment Company Act places significant restrictions on the types of transactions registered investment companies may undertake. Such companies are, for example, foreclosed from trading on margin or engaging in short sales, 15 U.S.C. § 80a-12(a)(1), (3), and must secure shareholder approval to take on significant debt or invest in certain types of assets, such as real estate or commodities, *id.* § 80a-13(a)(2). These transactions are all core elements of most hedge funds' trading strategies. "Hedging" transactions, from which the term "hedge fund" developed, involve taking both long and short positions on debt and equity securities to reduce risk. This is still the most frequently used hedge fund strategy, though there are many others. Hedge funds trade in all sorts of assets, from traditional stocks, bonds, and currencies to more exotic financial derivatives and even non-financial assets. Hedge funds often use leverage to increase their returns.

Another distinctive feature of hedge funds is their management structure. Unlike mutual funds, which must comply with detailed requirements for independent boards of directors, 15 U.S.C. § 80a-10, and whose shareholders must explicitly approve of certain actions, *id.* § 80a-13, domestic hedge funds are usually structured as limited partnerships to achieve maximum separation of ownership and management. In the typical arrangement, the general partner manages the fund (or several funds) for a fixed fee and a percentage of the gross profits from the fund. The limited partners are passive investors and generally take no part in management activities.

Hedge fund advisers also had been exempt from regulation under the Investment Advisers Act of 1940, 15 U.S.C. § 80b-1 *et seq.* ("Advisers Act"), a companion statute to the Investment Company Act, and the statute which primarily concerns us in this case. Enacted by Congress to "substitute a philosophy of full disclosure for the philosophy of *caveat emptor*" in the investment advisory profession, the Advisers Act is mainly a registration and anti-fraud statute. Non-exempt "investment advisers" must register with the Commission, 15 U.S.C. § 80b-3, and all advisers are prohibited from engaging in fraudulent or deceptive practices, *id.* § 80b-6. By keeping a census of advisers, the Commission can better respond to, initiate, and take remedial action on complaints against fraudulent advisers. *See id.* § 80b-4 (authorizing the Commission to examine registered advisers' records).

Hedge fund general partners meet the definition of "investment adviser" in the Advisers Act. *See* 15 U.S.C. § 80b-2(11) (defining "investment adviser" as one who "for compensation, engages in the business of advising others, either directly or through publications or writings, as to the value of securities or as to the advisability of investing in, purchasing, or selling securities"). But they usually satisfy the "private adviser exemption" from registration in § 203(b)(3) of the Act, 15 U.S.C. § 80b-3(b)(3). That section exempts "any investment adviser who during the course of the preceding twelve months has had fewer than fifteen clients and who neither holds himself out generally to the public as an investment adviser nor acts as an investment adviser to any investment company registered under [the Investment Company Act]." *Id.* As applied to limited partnerships and other entities, the Commission had interpreted this provision to refer to the partnership or entity itself as the adviser's "client." *See* 17 C.F.R. § 275.203(b)(3)-1. Even the largest hedge fund managers usually ran fewer than fifteen hedge funds and were therefore exempt.

Although the Commission has a history of interest in hedge funds, the current push for regulation had its origins in the failure of Long-Term Capital Management, a Greenwich, Connecticut-based fund that had more than $ 125 billion in assets under management at its peak. In late 1998, the fund nearly collapsed. Almost all of the country's major financial institutions were put at risk due to their credit exposure to Long-Term, and the president of the Federal Reserve Bank of New York personally intervened to engineer a bailout of the fund in order to avoid a national financial crisis.

A joint working group of the major federal financial regulators produced a report recommending regulatory changes to the regime governing hedge funds, and the Commission's staff followed with its own report about the state of hedge fund regulation. Drawing on the conclusions in the *Staff Report*, the Commission -- over the dissent of two of its members -- issued the rule under review in December 2004 after notice and comment. The Commission cited three recent shifts in the hedge fund industry to justify the need for increased regulation. First, despite the failure of Long-Term Capital Management, hedge fund assets grew by 260 percent from 1999 to 2004. Second, the Commission noticed a trend toward "retailization" of hedge funds that increased the exposure of ordinary investors to such funds. This retailization was driven by hedge funds loosening their investment requirements, the birth of "funds of hedge funds" that offered shares to the public, and increased investment in hedge funds by pension funds, universities, endowments, foundations and other charitable organizations. Third, the Commission was concerned about an increase in the number of fraud actions brought against hedge funds. Concluding that its "current regulatory program for hedge fund advisers [was] inadequate," the Commission moved to require hedge fund advisers to register under the Advisers Act so that it could gather "basic information about hedge fund advisers and the hedge fund industry," "oversee hedge fund advisers," and "deter or detect fraud by unregistered hedge fund advisers."

The *Hedge Fund Rule* first defines a "private fund" as an investment company that (a) is exempt from registration under the Investment Company Act by virtue of having fewer than one hundred investors or only qualified investors, *see* 15 U.S.C. § 80a-3(c)(1), (7); (b) permits its investors to redeem their interests within two years of investing; and (c) markets itself on the basis of the "skills, ability or expertise of the investment adviser." 17 C.F.R. § 275.203(b)(3)-1(d)(1). For these private funds, the rule then specifies that "[f]or purposes of section 203(b)(3) of the [Advisers] Act (15 U.S.C. § 80b-3(b)(3)), you must count as clients the shareholders, limited partners, members, or beneficiaries . . . of [the] fund." *Id.* § 275.203(b)(3)-2(a). The rule had the effect of requiring most hedge fund advisers to register by February 1, 2006.

II.

The dissenting Commissioners disputed the factual predicates for the new rule and its wisdom. Goldstein makes some of the same points but the major thrust of his complaint is that the Commission's action misinterpreted § 203(b)(3) of the Advisers Act, a charge the Commission dissenters also leveled. This provision exempts from registration "any investment adviser who during the course of the preceding twelve months has had fewer than fifteen *clients*." 15 U.S.C. § 80b-3(b)(3) (emphasis added). The Act does not define "client." Relying on *Chevron U.S.A. Inc. v. NRDC*, the Commission believes this renders the statute "ambiguous as to a method for counting clients." There is no such rule of law. The lack of a statutory definition of a word does not necessarily render the meaning of a word ambiguous, just as the presence of a definition does not necessarily make the meaning clear. A definition only pushes the problem back to the meaning of the defining terms.

If Congress employs a term susceptible of several meanings, as many terms are, it scarcely follows that Congress has authorized an agency to choose *any* one of those meanings. As always, the "words of the statute should be read in context, the statute's place in the overall statutory scheme should be considered, and the problem Congress sought to solve should be taken into account" to determine whether Congress has foreclosed the agency's interpretation.

"Client" may mean different things depending on context. The client of a laundry occupies a very different position than the client of a lawyer. Even for professional representation, the specific indicia of a client relationship -- contracts, fees, duties, and the like -- vary with the profession and with the particulars of the situation. An attorney-client relationship, for example, can be formed without any signs of formal "employment." Mattters may be very different for the client of, say, an architectural firm.

The Commission believes that an amendment to § 203(b)(3) suggests the possibility that an investor in a hedge fund could be counted as a client of the fund's adviser. In 1980, Congress added to § 203(b)(3) the following language: "For purposes of determining the number of clients of an investment adviser under this paragraph, no shareholder, partner, or beneficial owner of a business development company . . . shall be deemed to be a client of such investment adviser unless such person is a client of such investment adviser separate and apart from his status as a shareholder, partner, or beneficial owner." This language was inserted against a backdrop of uncertainty created by the Second Circuit's decision in *Abrahamson v. Fleschner*. The *Abrahamson* court held that hedge fund general partners were "investment advisers" under the Advisers Act. In its original opinion, the court specified that the general partners were advisers "to the limited partners." The final published opinion omits those four words, suggesting that the court expressly declined to resolve any ambiguity in the term "client." If -- as we generally assume -- Congress was aware of this judicial confusion, the 1980 amendment could be seen as Congress's acknowledgment that "client" is ambiguous in the context of § 203(b)(3). There are statements in the legislative history that suggest as much. *See, e.g.*, H.R. REP. NO. 96-1341, at 62 (1980) ("[W]ith respect to persons or firms which *do not* advise business development companies, the . . . amendment . . . is not intended to suggest that each shareholder, partner, or beneficial owner of a company advised by such person or firm *should or should not be* regarded as a client . . .." (emphasis added)). Although "the views of a subsequent Congress form a hazardous basis for inferring the intent of an earlier one," the 1980 amendment might be seen as introducing another definitional possibility into the statute.

On the other hand, a 1970 amendment to § 203 appears to reflect Congress's understanding at the time that investment company entities, not their shareholders, were the advisers' clients. In the amendment, Congress eliminated a separate exemption from registration for advisers who advised only investment companies and explicitly made the fewer-than-fifteen-clients exemption unavailable to such advisers. This latter prohibition would have been unnecessary if the shareholders of investment companies could be counted as "clients."

Another section of the Advisers Act strongly suggests that Congress did not intend "shareholders, limited partners, members, or beneficiaries" of a hedge fund to be counted as "clients." Although the statute does not define "client," it does define "investment adviser" as "any person who, for compensation, engages in the business of advising others, either *directly* or through publications or writings, as to the value of securities or as to the advisability of investing in, purchasing, or selling securities." 15 U.S.C. § 80b-2(11) (emphasis added). An investor in a private fund may benefit from the adviser's advice (or he may suffer from it) but he does not receive the advice *directly*. He invests a portion of his assets in the fund. The fund manager -- the adviser -- controls the disposition of the pool of capital in the fund. The adviser does not tell the *investor* how to spend his money; the investor made that decision when he invested in the fund. Having bought into the fund, the investor fades into the background; his role is completely passive. If the person or entity controlling the fund is not an "investment adviser" to each individual investor, then *a fortiori* each investor cannot be a "client" of that person or entity. These are just two sides of the same coin.

This had been the Commission's view until it issued the new rule. As recently as 1997, it explained that a "client of an investment adviser typically is provided with individualized advice that is based on the client's financial situation and investment objectives. In contrast, the investment adviser of an investment company need not consider the individual needs of the company's shareholders when making investment decisions, and thus has no obligation to ensure that each security purchased for the company's portfolio is an appropriate investment for each shareholder." The Commission said much the same in 1985 when it promulgated a rule with respect to investment companies set up as limited partnerships rather than as corporations. The "client" for purposes of the fifteen-client rule of § 203(b)(3) is the limited partnership not the individual partners. *See* 17 C.F.R. § 275.203(b)(3)-1(a)(2). As the Commission wrote in proposing the rule, when "an adviser to an investment pool manages the assets of the pool on the basis of the investment objectives of the participants as a group, it appears appropriate to view the pool -- rather than each participant -- as a client of the adviser."

The Supreme Court embraced a similar conception of the adviser-client relationship when it held in *Lowe v. SEC* that publishers of certain financial newsletters were not "investment advisers." After an extensive discussion of the legislative history of the Advisers Act, the Court held that existence of an advisory relationship depended largely on the character of the advice rendered. Persons engaged in the investment advisory profession "provide personalized advice attuned to a client's concerns." "[F]iduciary, person-to-person relationships" were "characteristic" of the "investment adviser-client relationship[]." The Court thought it "significant" that the Advisers Act "repeatedly" referred to "clients," which signified to the Court "the kind of fiduciary relationship the Act was designed to regulate." This type of direct relationship exists between the adviser and the fund, but not between the adviser and the investors in the fund. The adviser is concerned with the fund's performance, not with each investor's financial condition.

The Commission nevertheless is right to point out that the *Lowe* Court was not rendering an interpretation of the word "client." Because it was construing an exception to the definition of "investment adviser," we do not read too much into the Court's understanding of the meaning of "client."

As we have noted before, "[i]t may be that . . . the strict dichotomy between clarity and ambiguity is artificial, that what we have is a continuum, a probability of meaning." Here, even if the Advisers Act does not foreclose the Commission's interpretation, the interpretation falls outside the bounds of reasonableness. "An agency construction of a statute cannot survive judicial review if a contested regulation reflects an action that exceeds the agency's authority. It does not matter whether the unlawful action arises because the disputed regulation defies the plain language of a statute or because the agency's construction is utterly unreasonable and thus impermissible."

"The 'reasonableness' of an agency's construction depends," in part, "on the construction's 'fit' with the statutory language, as well as its conformity to statutory purposes." As described above, the Commission's interpretation of the word "client" comes close to violating the plain language of the statute. At best it is counterintuitive to characterize the investors in a hedge fund as the "clients" of the adviser. The adviser owes fiduciary duties only to the fund, not to the fund's investors. Section 206 of the Advisers Act, 15 U.S.C. § 80b-6, makes it unlawful for any investment adviser -- registered or not -- "to engage in any transaction, practice, or course of business which operates as a fraud or deceit upon any client or prospective client." *Id.* § 80b-6(2). In *SEC v. Capital Gains Research Bureau, Inc.*, the Supreme Court held that this provision created a fiduciary duty of loyalty between an adviser and his client. ("The statute, in recognition of the adviser's fiduciary relationship to his clients, requires that his advice be disinterested."). In that case, the duty of loyalty required an adviser to disclose self-interested transactions to his clients. The Commission recognizes more generally that the duty of loyalty "requires advisers to manage their clients' portfolios in the best interest of clients," and imposes obligations to "fully disclose any material conflicts the adviser has with its clients, to seek best execution for client transactions, and to have a reasonable basis for client recommendations."

If the investors are owed a fiduciary duty and the entity is also owed a fiduciary duty, then the adviser will inevitably face conflicts of interest. Consider an investment adviser to a hedge fund that is about to go bankrupt. His advice to the fund will likely include any and all measures to remain solvent. His advice to an investor in the fund, however, would likely be to sell. For the same reason, we do not ordinarily deem the shareholders in a corporation the "clients" of the corporation's lawyers or accountants. While the shareholders may benefit from the professionals' counsel indirectly, their individual interests easily can be drawn into conflict with the interests of the entity. It simply cannot be the case that investment advisers are the servants of two masters in this way.

The Commission's response to this argument is telling. It argues that the *Hedge Fund Rule* amends *only* the method for counting clients under § 203(b)(3), and that it does not "alter the duties or obligations owed by an investment adviser to its clients." We ordinarily presume that the same words used in different parts of a statute have the same meaning. The Commission cannot explain why "client" should mean one thing when determining to whom fiduciary duties are owed, 15 U.S.C. § 80b-6(1)-(3), and something else entirely when determining whether an investment adviser must register under the Act, *id.* § 80b-3(b)(3).

The Commission also argues that the organizational form of most hedge funds is merely "legal artifice," to shield advisers who want to advise more than fifteen clients and remain exempt from registration. But as the discussion above shows, form matters in this area of the law because it dictates to whom fiduciary duties are owed.

The *Hedge Fund Rule* might be more understandable if, over the years, the advisory relationship between hedge fund advisers and investors had changed. The Commission cited, as justification for its rule, a rise in the amount of hedge fund assets, indications that more pension funds and other institutions were investing in hedge funds, and an increase in fraud actions involving hedge funds. All of this may be true, although the dissenting Commissioners doubted it. But without any evidence that the role of fund advisers with respect to investors had undergone a transformation, there is a disconnect between the factors the Commission cited and the rule it promulgated. That the Commission wanted a hook on which to hang more comprehensive regulation of hedge funds may be understandable. But the Commission may not accomplish its objective by a manipulation of meaning.

The Commission has, in short, not adequately explained how the relationship between hedge fund investors and advisers justifies treating the former as clients of the latter. The Commission points to its finding that a hedge fund adviser sometimes "may not treat all of its hedge fund investors the same." From this the Commission concludes that each account of a hedge fund investor "*may* bear many of the characteristics of separate investment accounts, which, of course, must be counted as separate clients." But the Commission's conclusion does not follow from its premise. It may be that different classes of investors have different rights or privileges with respect to their investments. This reveals little, however, about the *relationship* between the investor and the adviser. Even if it did, the Commission has not justified treating *all* investors in hedge funds as clients for the purpose of the rule. If there are certain characteristics present in some investor-adviser relationships that mark a "client" relationship, then the Commission should have identified those characteristics and tailored its rule accordingly.

By painting with such a broad brush, the Commission has failed adequately to justify departing from its own prior interpretation of § 203(b)(3). As we have discussed, in 1985 the Commission adopted a "safe harbor" for general partners of limited partnerships, enabling them to count the partnership as a single "client" for the purposes of § 203 so long as they provided advice to a "collective investment vehicle" based on the investment objectives of the limited partners as a group. This "safe harbor" remains part of the Commission's rules and has since been expanded to include corporations, limited liability companies, and business trusts (hedge funds sometimes take these less common forms). The *Hedge Fund Rule* therefore appears to carve out an exception from this safe harbor solely for investment entities that have fewer than one hundred-one but more than fourteen investors. *Compare* 17 C.F.R. § 275.203(b)(3)-1, *with id.* § 275.203(b)(3)-2. As discussed above, the Commission does not justify this exception by reference to any change in the nature of investment adviser-client relationships since the safe harbor was adopted. Absent such a justification, its choice appears completely arbitrary.

Nor is this choice any more rational when viewed in light of the policy goals underlying the Advisers Act. The Commission recites Congress's findings in § 201 that investment advisory activities "substantially . . . affect . . . national securities exchanges . . . and the national economy," 15 U.S.C. § 80b-1(3), and concludes that "[i]n enacting [section 203(b)(3)], Congress exempted from the registration requirements a category of advisers whose activities were not sufficiently large or national in scope." The Commission reasons that because hedge funds are now national in scope, treating the entity as a single client for the purpose of the exemption would frustrate Congress's policy. If Congress did intend the exemption to prevent regulation only of small-scale operations -- a policy goal that is clear from neither the statute's text nor its legislative history -- the Commission's rule bears no rational relationship to achieving that goal. The number of investors in a hedge fund -- the "clients" according to the Commission's rule -- reveals nothing about the scale or scope of the fund's activities. It is the volume of assets under management or the extent of indebtedness of a hedge fund or other such financial metrics that determines a fund's importance to national markets. One might say that if Congress meant to exclude regulation of small operations, it chose a very odd way of accomplishing its objective -- by excluding investment companies with one hundred or fewer investors and investment advisers having fewer than fifteen clients. But the *Hedge Fund Rule* only exacerbates whatever problems one might perceive in Congress's method for determining who to regulate. The Commission's rule creates a situation in which funds with one hundred or fewer investors are exempt from the more demanding Investment Company Act, but those with fifteen or more investors trigger registration under the Advisers Act. This is an arbitrary rule.

*　　*　　*

The petition for review is granted, and the *Hedge Fund Rule* is vacated and remanded.

*　　*　　*

Page 278. After the first full paragraph ("Our compliance . . .") and before the notes, insert the following"

Martin E. Lybecker,
**Enhanced Corporate Governance for Mutual Funds:
A Flawed Concept that Deserves Serious Reconsideration**
83 Wash. U. L. Rev. 1045 (2005) *

Introduction

Mutual funds are the most popular retail investment in America, a testament to the simplicity and transparency of the mutual fund concept. A mutual fund investor owns a share of common stock issued by a company that invests in debt or equity securities issued by other, operating companies. Like operating companies, a mutual fund distinguishes itself by its business objective -- for example, to exceed the Standard & Poor's 500 Index [an equity fund], to match the Lehman Brothers Aggregate Bond Index [a bond fund], or to maintain a current net asset value per share of $1.00 [a money market fund]. Unlike an operating company that is managed by its officers and employees, most mutual funds are managed by an external investment adviser pursuant to a contract. In recognition of the obvious conflict of interest between a mutual fund and its investment adviser because of that contract, the Investment Company Act in 1940 ("Investment Company Act") has always required that no less than 40% of the members of the mutual fund's board of directors be independent. In July 2004, the Securities and Exchange Commission ("SEC" or "Commission"), in a 3-to-2 vote, amended certain existing exemptive rules (the "Corporate Governance Amendments") to require that no less than 75% of the members of a mutual fund's board of directors be independent, that the chairman of the board of directors be an independent director, and that the board of directors engage in certain specific corporate governance practices. This Article will argue that the Commission's decision to adopt the Corporate Governance Amendments was without statutory authority and usurped the proper legislative role of Congress, was not adequately justified, and will be of questionable efficacy.

I. The Evolving Corporate Governance Regulatory Framework for Mutual Funds

A. The 1940 Act as a Baseline for Comparison

The original Senate bill that would ultimately become the Investment Company Act would have required that a majority of the members of a mutual fund's board of directors be independent. However, Congress ultimately provided that 40% of the members of a mutual fund's board of directors be independent. Congress believed that investors would prefer to choose mutual funds that they knew would be guided principally by individuals affiliated with the mutual fund's investment adviser.

---

* Martin E. Lybecker is a partner of Wilmer Cutler Pickering Hale and Dorr LLP, located in Washington, D.C., and is a Senior Lecturing Fellow in Law at Duke University. Wilmer Cutler Pickering Hale and Dorr LLP represents or has represented some of the entities mentioned in this Article. [Footnotes omitted.]

"The bill as originally introduced . . . required that a majority of the board be independent of the management. However, the argument was made that it is difficult for a person or firm to undertake the management of an investment company, [and] give advice, when the majority of the board may repudiate that advice. It was urged that if a person is buying management of a particular person and if the majority of the board can repudiate his advice, then in effect, you are depriving the stockholders of that person's advice. . . . [T]hat is why the provision for 40 percent of independents was inserted."

Importantly, Congress also simultaneously provided different formulas regarding membership on a mutual fund's board of directors to address different situations:

- A majority of the members may not be affiliated persons of a regular broker, an underwriter, or an investment banker if the mutual fund employs as a regular broker, underwriter, or investment banker any director, officer, or employee of the mutual fund, or any person of which such any such person is an affiliated person;
- A majority of the members may not be persons who are officers, directors, or employees of any bank; and
- Only one independent director is necessary if the mutual fund is no-load, its investment adviser's fee does not exceed 1% of assets under management, and the mutual fund has only one class of securities outstanding.

The point is that even in 1940 Congress had definite, nuanced ideas about the composition of a mutual fund's board of directors. It also bears emphasis that Congress did not in 1940 elect to legislate about any other matter of corporate governance, with the result that mutual funds have always looked to corporate law in the jurisdiction in which they are organized to determine all kinds of routine corporate matters.

B. The 1970 Amendments Act

In 1970, new Section 15(c) was added to the Investment Company Act and Section 2(a)(19) was amended by the Investment Company Amendments Act of 1970 ("1970 Amendments Act"). Section 15(c) provides that:

"[(1) [I]t shall be unlawful for any [mutual fund] having a board of directors to enter into, renew, or perform any contract or agreement, written or oral, whereby a person undertakes regularly to serve or act as investment adviser of or principal underwriter for such [mutual fund], unless the terms of such contract or agreement and any renewal thereof have been approved by the vote of a majority of directors, who are not parties to such contract or agreement or interested persons of any such party, cast in person at a meeting called for the purpose of voting on such approval. [(2)] It shall be the duty of the directors of a [mutual fund] to request and evaluate, and the duty of an investment adviser to furnish, such information as may reasonably be necessary to evaluate the terms of any contract whereby a person undertakes regularly to serve or act as investment adviser of such [mutual fund]."

The purpose of Section 15(c) was to empower the independent members of the board of directors of a mutual fund (1) by requiring that the investment advisory contract be approved by a majority of independent directors at an in-person meeting, and (2) by giving them the statutory authority to demand information and to impose on the investment adviser the obligation to provide it. It is notable that the Congressional draftsmen of Section 15(c) chose to empower <u>all</u> of the directors of a mutual fund, not just those who are independent, suggesting that an interested director of a mutual fund has the same fiduciary obligations as an independent director of a mutual fund with respect to review and approval of the mutual fund's investment advisory contract.

Section (2)(19) was amended by the 1970 Amendments Act to provide that:

"Interested person of another person means -- (A) when used with respect to an investment company --

(i) any affiliated person of such company,

(ii) any member of the immediate family of any natural person who is an affiliated person of such company,

(iii) any interested person of any investment adviser of or principal underwriter for such company,

(iv) any person or partner or employee of any person who at any time since the beginning of the last two completed fiscal years of such company has acted as legal counsel for such company,

(v) an natural person whom the Commission by order shall have determined to be an interested person by reason of having had, at any time since the beginning of the last two completed fiscal years of such company, a material business or professional relationship with such company or with the principal executive officer of such company or with any other investment company having the same investment adviser or principal underwriter or with the principal executive officer of such other investment company:

"*Provided*, that no person shall be deemed to be an interested person of an investment company solely by reason of (aa) his being a member of its board of directors or advisory board or an owner of its securities, or (bb) his membership in the immediate family of any person specified in clause (aa) of this proviso ...."

Section 2(a)(19) casts a very wide net, precluding virtually any one with a business or professional relationship with the mutual fund or its investment adviser from serving as an independent director of the mutual fund.

Section 2(a)(19) was amended in 1999 by the Gramm-Leach-Bliley Act by adding new clauses (v) and (vi) and renumbering old clause (v) to become clause (vii). New clauses (v) and (vi) add to the term "interested person" a person who at any time within the 6-month period preceding the date of the determination has executed portfolio transactions for or engaged in any principal transactions with, or distributed shares for the investment company, and a person who at any time within the 6-month period preceding the date of the determination was loaned money or other property to the investment company. The purpose of the Gramm-Leach-Bliley Act amendments was to reflect the fact that a broker-dealer or bank could serve as an investment adviser to a mutual fund and disallow persons who were affiliated with a broker-dealer or bank otherwise doing business with a mutual fund from serving as an independent director of that mutual fund.

C. The 1975 Amendments Act

In 1975, new Section 15(f) was added to the Investment Company Act by the Securities Acts Amendments Act of 1975 ("1975 Amendments Act"). Section 15(f)(1) provides that:

> "An investment adviser ... of a [mutual fund] or an affiliated person of such investment adviser ... may receive any amount or benefit in connection with a sale of securities or, or a sale of any other interest in, such investment adviser ... which results in an assignment of an investment advisory contract with such [mutual fund] ... if:

> "(A) For a period of three years after the time of such action, at least 75 percent of the members of the board of directors of such [mutual fund] ... are not: (i) interested persons of the investment adviser of such [mutual fund] ... , or (ii) interested persons of the predecessor investment adviser ... ; and

> "(B) There is not imposed an unfair unburden on such [mutual fund] as a result of such transaction or any express or implied terms, conditions, or undertakings applicable thereto...."

Section 15(f) was adopted by Congress in response to the decision of the U.S. Court of Appeals for the Second Circuit in *Rosenfeld v. Black*, in which the Second Circuit ruled that an investment adviser to a closed-end fund that sold its investment advisory contract to a third-party -- which would succeed it as investment adviser to the closed-end fund -- had breached its fiduciary duty to the closed-end fund in that the investment advisory contract with the closed-end fund was an asset of the closed-end fund (and not the investment adviser's) that the investment adviser could not lawfully sell. There was a strong reaction to the *Rosenfeld* decision for, if applied literally to investment advisers to mutual funds, it would deprive them of one traditional avenue of capturing the value of the business that had been built up over the years by selling the stock of the investment adviser to a successor investment adviser. Section 15(f) resolved the uncertainty caused by the *Rosenfeld* decision by allowing the sale of the investment advisory contract while adding two principal safeguards to protect a mutual fund and its shareholders -- the requirement that 75% of the members of the board of directors be independent for at least three years, and the requirement that the transaction not impose any unfair burden on the investment company.

D. Rule 12b-1 in 1980

Rule 12b-1 was adopted in 1980 after a long period of consideration by the Commission regarding whether assets of mutual funds should be used to make payments to selling dealers to supplement the process of distributing shares of mutual funds. Before the mid-1970s, most mutual funds were sold with a sales load or were "no-load" and the sponsor/principal underwriter/investment adviser to the mutual fund borne the cost of distributing shares of the no-load mutual fund. It was the advent of money market funds and the introduction of broker-dealer sponsored "cash management accounts" in the mid-1970s that caused concern regarding the process of distribution. Shares of a money market fund, offering a stable net asset value of $1.00 with a return based on its portfolio of high-quality, short-term debt securities, could scarcely be sold with a sales load (although the very earliest versions were sold with a low-load); a brokerage account with "sweep" capability, daily redemptions, wire transfers, and check-writing privileges (providing the functionality of a bank time deposit offering an interest rate that varies daily with the money markets), could not bear the costs of sales loads on daily transactions.

After strongly resisting the idea of allowing a mutual fund's assets to be used to pay for the distribution of its shares, the SEC ultimately decided to adopt Rule 12b-1 to require such payments to be subject to annual review and approval by the mutual fund's board of directors. For this purpose, as adopted in 1980 paragraph (c) of Rule 12b-1 allowed a mutual fund to rely on Rule 12b-1 only if a majority of the members of the mutual fund's board of directors were independent, and those independent directors selected and nominated all other independent members of the mutual fund's board of directors. Interestingly, much of the adopting release is devoted to arguments that the Commission had the statutory authority in Section 12(b) to regulate the use of fund assets to pay for distribution, and that it was proper to include indirect distribution expenses within Rule 12b-1 so that all distribution expenses knowingly financed by a mutual fund's board of directors would fall within the ambit of Rule 12b-1. The SEC's final position was that, where an investment adviser bears distribution expenses out of its own resources, the investment advisory fee must not be a conduit for the indirect use of fund assets; in other words, if the investment advisory fee is not "excessive" within the meaning of Section 36(b) (*e.g.* they are "legitimate profits"), the distribution expenses borne by the investment adviser are not an indirect use of a mutual fund's assets.

E. "Protecting Investors" -- The Special Study in 1992

In 1992, the SEC's Division of Investment Management issued its important study, "Protecting Investors: A Half Century of Investment Company Regulation." Chapter 7 of the study was devoted to "investment company governance." The Division concluded that:

> "[t]he governance model embodied in the [Investment Company] Act is sound and should be retained, with limited modifications. The oversight function performed by [mutual fund] boards of directors, especially the 'watchdog' function performed by the independent directors, has served investors well, at minimal cost. In our view, however, the increasingly significant responsibilities placed on independent directors warrant a few changes to further strengthen their independence. Accordingly, the Division recommends that the Commission recommend legislation that would increase the minimum proportion of independent directors on [mutual fund] boards from forty percent to more than fifty percent. In addition, the Division recommends that independent director vacancies be filled by person chosen by remaining independent directors. Finally, the Division proposes

that independent directors be given the express authority to terminate advisory contracts.

"At the same time, however, the Division recommends eliminating provisions in certain rules under the [Investment Company] Act that make independent directors responsible for detailed findings of fact or for reviews and findings that involve more ritual than substance. Elimination of such formalistic requirements will increase the effectiveness of boards of directors by allowing them to focus to a greater extent on what they do best -- exercising business judgment in their review of interested party transactions and in their oversight of operational matters where the interests of a[] [mutual fund] and its adviser may diverge."

The recommendations from this important study are striking in at least two respects: (i) the Division expected Congress (and not the Commission through rulemaking) to effect any change in the minimum percent of members on a mutual fund's board of directors who must be independent; and (ii) the Division believed that the highest and best use of independent directors was review of interested party transactions and other matters where the interests of the mutual fund and its adviser might diverge.

F. The 2001 Amendments

In 1999, the Commission convened a two-day public Roundtable on the Role of Independent Investment Company Directors to discuss the role of independent directors and the steps that could be taken to improve their effectiveness. Based on this record, the Commission proposed that independent directors constitute a majority of the board of directors of a mutual fund relying on certain exemptive rules, that legal counsel to independent directors be independent, and that independent directors nominate and select new independent directors. With respect to the requirement that independent directors have "independent legal counsel," if they have any counsel at all, Rule 0-1(a)(6)(i) under the Investment Company Act provides that a person is "independent legal counsel" with respect to the independent directors of a mutual fund if:

"(A) A majority of the [independent] directors determine in the exercise of their judgment (and record the basis for that determination in the minutes of their meeting) and that representation by the person of the [mutual fund]'s investment adviser, principal underwriter, administrator ("management organizations"), or any of their control persons, since the beginning of the [mutual] fund's last two completed fiscal years, is or was sufficiently limited that it is unlikely to adversely affect the professional judgment of the person in providing legal representation to the [independent] directors; and

"(B) The [independent] directors have obtained an undertaking from such person to provide them with information necessary to make their determination and to update promptly that information when the person begins to represent, or materially increases his representation of, a management organization or control person."

In January 2001, the Commission adopted the 2001 Amendments.

The 2001 Amendments were just as extralegal as the Corporate Governance Amendments are, but were less controversial or intrusive because (a) many mutual funds had adopted Plans pursuant to Rule 12b-1 and thus at least 50% of the members of the board of directors were already independent, and (b) most independent directors were already represented by legal counsel who were independent in that they did not also represent the mutual fund's investment adviser.

II. The Scandals from 2003-2004

A. Market-Timing

On September 3, 2003, the New York Attorney General announced a civil injunctive action against Canary Capital Partners LLC ("Canary Capital") in which Canary Capital agreed to pay $40 million to settle claims against it under the Martin Act. The Canary Capital complaint described four mutual fund groups that had cooperated with Canary Capital by, *inter alia*, allegedly allowing it to effect market-timing and "late-trading" transactions in shares of certain mutual funds in return for "sticky assets" (usually invested in a private hedge fund also managed by the investment adviser); one of the investment advisers allegedly effectively functioned as Canary Capital's prime broker, lent it money, allowed a terminal to be installed in Canary Capital's offices to facilitate late trading in shares of mutual funds, and disclosed portfolio holdings to, and designed derivative instruments for, Canary Capital to permit it to consummate more efficient hedging transactions based on the non-public information about the mutual fund's investment portfolio.

Mutual funds are required by Rule 22c-1 under the Investment Company Act to effect transactions in their shares at the current net asset value per share ("NAV") next determined after receipt of the request for redemption or order to purchase. Most mutual funds calculate their NAV at 4:00 pm Eastern Time, so orders received after 4:00 pm Eastern Time today should be effected at the price next determined, *e.g.* the NAV calculated at 4:00 pm tomorrow. Section 2(a)(41)(B) of the Investment Company Act defines the term "value" to mean (i) with respect to securities for which market quotations are readily available, the market value of such securities, and (ii) with respect to other securities and assets, fair value as determined in good faith by the board of directors. Among other things, Canary Capital was exploiting anomalies in the price for securities held by global funds where a significant event had occurred after the market had closed in London or the Far East (*e.g.* there was a market quotation that was readily available from earlier in the day but it had become "stale" as a result of events that occurred after the market had closed), or was effecting trades after 4:00 pm Eastern Time ("late-trading") when a significant event had occurred in the U.S. markets after the U.S. markets had closed. Arguably, the former problem could be "cured" if the board of directors of a mutual fund were to "fair value" the portfolio securities held by global or international funds before the NAV is calculated at 4:00 pm Eastern Time where their prices have become "stale;" there is no "cure" for trades illegally entered after 4:00 pm without the knowledge of the mutual fund (and/or its service providers) other than the pursuit of civil and criminal actions against the lawbreakers after the fact.

Since the announcement of the Canary Capital settlement, a number of enforcement cases have been brought against mutual fund advisers and broker-dealers under the Investment Company Act, the Securities Act of 1933 ("1933 Act"), the Securities Exchange Act of 1934 ("Exchange Act"), the Investment Advisers Act of 1940 ("Advisers Act"), NASD rules, and state securities laws brought by the SEC, NASD, and the attorneys general of a number of states. To date, most of the settled cases involve alleged charges that the investment adviser breached its fiduciary duty under the Advisers Act by allowing market-timing transactions to occur notwithstanding disclosure in the affected mutual fund's prospectus that market-timing transactions were prohibited or severely restricted. None of the settled cases involve alleged charges against members of the mutual fund's board of directors who were independent -- instead, there is usually an allegation that the investment adviser failed to inform the mutual fund's board of directors of the precise nature of the market-timing activities that it was allowing to occur.

To address these issues, the Commission has adopted amendments to Form N-1A to require enhanced disclosure of a mutual fund's risks, policies, and procedures concerning market-timing, selective disclosure of portfolio holdings, and the use of "fair value" pricing. The Commission also proposed amendments to Rule 22c-1 that would provide that, for an order to purchase or redeem shares to receive the NAV calculated by the mutual fund for today, the designated transfer agent or registered clearing agency must receive the order by the time that the mutual fund establishes for calculating its NAV. To bring previously unregulated hedge fund advisers into its regulatory fold, the Commission adopted Rule 203(b)(2)-2 under the Advisers Act redefining the term "client" in order to require certain investment advisers to hedge funds and other private investment companies to register under Section 203(c) of the Advisers Act notwithstanding the exception to registration in Section 203(b)(3) thereof for an investment adviser that is not holding itself out to the public and has fewer than 15 clients. Finally, the SEC proposed that mutual funds must impose a mandatory redemption fee of 2%, payable to the mutual fund, if an investor engages in rapid trading, and in March 2005 the Commission adopted new Rule 22c-2 authorizing (but not requiring) a mutual fund to impose a redemption fee of up to 2% upon shares that are sold within seven days of purchase.

B. Revenue-Sharing

In November 2003, the SEC and NASD settled cases against Morgan Stanley DW Inc. ("Morgan Stanley") for allegedly failing to disclose to its brokerage customers that it had had a Preferred Partners Program since 2002 in which its registered representatives were paid higher commissions and received other, extra compensation from Morgan Stanley and from the mutual fund advisers in the Preferred Partners Program for selling shares of the mutual funds in the Preferred Partners Program. Specifically, it was alleged that twelve third-party mutual fund complexes paid Morgan Stanley 15 or 20 basis points on gross sales of mutual fund shares, and 5 basis points on "aged assets," *e.g.* mutual fund shares held for more than one year. The 5 basis point component of the Preferred Partners Program was paid to the participating registered representatives, who also received a higher commission payout for selling mutual funds in the Preferred Partners Program than for other mutual funds. "Revenue-sharing" payments made by an investment adviser out of its own pocket are not subject to Rule 12b-1 under the Investment Company Act.

Rule 10b-10 under the Exchange Act requires the disclosure of certain information to a broker-dealer's customer on the confirmation statement, including "[t]he source and amount of any other remuneration received or to be received by the broker in connection with the transaction." In 1977 when adopting Rule 10b-10, the Commission stated that if the required information is set forth in a final prospectus delivered to the customer at the time of the transaction, then a broker-dealer need not provide the information separately on the confirmation. Nonetheless, to address this aspect of the Morgan Stanley case the Commission has proposed to amend the requirements of Form N-1A (the form for registering mutual funds under the 1933 Act and the Investment Company Act) to require increased disclosure of the investment adviser's "revenue-sharing" payments, and has proposed new Rules 15c2-2 and 15c2-3 under the Exchange Act and proposed amendments to Rule 10b-10 to require improved confirmation disclosure for transactions in mutual fund shares and point of sale disclosure prior to effecting transactions in mutual fund shares.

Since the announcement of the Morgan Stanley settlement, the SEC and NASD have brought several enforcement cases against mutual fund advisers and broker-dealers regarding "revenue-sharing." To date, virtually all of the settled cases involve allegations that the investment adviser breached its fiduciary duty by using fund assets to pay for distribution of mutual fund shares outside of a properly adopted Rule 12b-1 Plan notwithstanding general disclosure in the affected mutual fund's prospectus that "revenue-sharing" payments were being made by the mutual fund's investment adviser, or that the broker-dealer failed adequately to disclose its conflicts of interest with sufficient specificity to the brokerage customer at the point of sale. None of the settled cases involve charges against members of the mutual fund's board of directors who were independent -- instead, there is usually an allegation that the investment adviser failed to inform the mutual fund's board of directors of the precise nature of the "revenue-sharing" activities in which it was engaging.

C. Directed Brokerage

Some investment advisers used the brokerage commissions incurred in effecting securities transactions for the mutual fund to make "revenue-sharing" payments to Morgan Stanley. With respect to the receipt of payments by a broker-dealer in the form of brokerage commissions, before the Morgan Stanley case NASD Rule 2830(k) had prohibited a member broker-dealer from:

(1) favoring or disfavoring the sale of distribution of shares of any particular mutual fund or group of mutual funds on the basis of brokerage commissions received or expected by the member from any source,

(2) demanding or requiring brokerage commissions from any source as a condition to the sale or distribution of shares of a mutual fund,

(3) offering or promising to another member brokerage commissions from any source as a condition to the sale or distribution of shares of a mutual fund,

and requesting or arranging for the direction to any member of a specific amount of percentage of brokerage commissions conditioned upon that member's sales or promise of sales of shares of a mutual fund,

(4) circulating any information regarding the amount of level of brokerage commissions received by the member from any mutual fund to other than management personnel who are required, in the overall management of the member's business, to have access to such information,

(5) sponsoring any incentive campaign or special sales effort of another member with respect to the shares of a mutual fund which incentive or sales effort is to be based upon, or financed by, brokerage commissions directed or arranged by the underwriter-member, or

(6) providing incentive or additional compensation to salesmen, branch managers, or other sales personnel based on the amount of brokerage commissions received or expected, recommending specific mutual funds to sales personnel or establishing "selected" or "preferred" lists of mutual funds if such funds are recommended or selected on the basis of brokerage commissions received or expected from any source, granting any participation in brokerage commissions to salesmen, branch managers, or other sales personnel received by the member from portfolio transactions of a mutual fund, or using sales of shares of a mutual fund as a factor in negotiating the price or amount of brokerage commissions to be paid on a portfolio transaction for a mutual fund.

If all of these conditions could be met, then it was permissible (A) for a member to execute portfolio transactions of a mutual fund where the member also sells shares of the mutual fund, (B) where the mutual fund discloses in its prospectus that the consideration of sales of shares of the mutual fund is a factor in the selection of broker-dealers to execute brokerage transactions subject to the requirements of best execution, and (C) where the member compensates its salesmen and managers in a manner that is not designed to favor or disfavor sales of any particular mutual fund on a basis prohibited by the other provisions of Rule 2830(k).

To address this aspect of the Morgan Stanley case, the Commission has amended Rule 12b-1 by adding new paragraph (h) which prohibits a mutual fund from making "revenue-sharing" payments with brokerage commissions unless the mutual fund has implemented policies and procedures designed to ensure that the mutual fund adviser's selection of selling brokers to execute portfolio securities transactions is not influenced by considerations about the sale of fund shares. The NASD also amended its Rule 2830(k) to prohibit a broker-dealer from selling a mutual fund's shares if the broker-dealer has any agreement or understanding with any party that portfolio transactions will be directed to the member in exchange for the promotion or sale of fund shares, which the Commission promptly approved.

D. Some Thoughts on the Scandals

The facts described in the Canary Capital complaint were both astonishing and appalling. The settlements, uniformly harsh, reflect the Commission's own deep disappointment with those in the securities industry who violated or facilitated violation of the letter and spirit of Rule 22c-1 for personal gain and in any event to the disadvantage of mutual fund shareholders. The terms of the SEC market-timing settlements involving mutual fund advisers usually require, *inter alia*, that the board of directors of the effected mutual fund adopt a number of corporate governance changes that substantially mirror the Corporate Governance Amendments. The settlements also uniformly invoke the Fair Fund provisions in Section 308(a) of the Sarbanes-Oxley Act to provide for a master to administer and dispense the funds deposited in the Fair Fund, consisting of both the amount to be disgorged and the civil money penalty. Finally, the settlement usually requires the investment adviser to employ an independent consultant to review its compliance with the Federal securities laws and render reports to the Commission on specified dates.

With respect to revenue-sharing, it was generally believed that the Commission was well aware of mutual fund marketplaces and concepts like "shelf space" through inspections of investment advisers and broker-dealers, processing mutual fund registration statements, and its involvement in private appellate litigation regarding these activities. Accordingly, the Morgan Stanley enforcement case can be viewed as representing a significant change of position on the Commission's part. Unlike the market-timing settlements, several of the "revenue-sharing" settlements require disgorgement of only $1, with a substantial civil money penalty, solely to invoke the use of a Fair Fund to administer receipt and disbursal of the civil money penalty.

III. Adoption of the Corporate Governance Amendments in 2004

A. The SEC's Preliminary Thoughts

In adopting the Corporate Governance Amendments, the Commission made several preliminary observations about the role of independent directors. First, the Commission focused on the central role that independent directors play in policing the conflicts of interest that advisers inevitably have with the mutual funds that they advise, asserting that to be truly effective a mutual fund's board of directors must be an independent force in the mutual fund's affairs. Second, the Commission described the operation of Section 15(c), and stated that the best way to ensure that mutual fund shareholders obtain fair and reasonable fees is through a marketplace of vigorous, independent, and diligent mutual fund boards of directors coupled with fully-informed investors. Finally, the Commission discussed the process of selecting and nominating new independent directors, and encouraged the selection of persons with the background, experience, and independent judgment to represent the interests of mutual fund investors.

B. 75% Independence Requirement

The Corporate Governance Amendments require that at least 75% of the members of a mutual fund's board of directors be independent. The Commission asserts that a principal purpose is to strengthen the independent directors' control of the mutual fund's board of directors and its agenda, citing the 75% requirement in Section 15(f) as appropriate to assure that the independent directors can carry out their fiduciary requirements. The Commission also asserts that the investment adviser controls the day-to-day activities of the mutual fund and has significant greater access to information about the mutual fund than do the independent directors, and the 75% independence requirement seeks to resolve this imbalance.

C. Independent Chairman Requirement

The Corporate Governance Amendments require that the chairman of the board of directors be an independent director. Citing the scandals discussed above, the Commission asserted that a mutual fund's board of directors is in a better position to protect the interests of the mutual fund, and to fulfill the board's obligations under the Investment Company Act, when its chairman does not have the conflicts of interest inherent in the role of an executive of the investment adviser. The Commission commented that a board chairman can: (i) play an important role in setting the agenda of the board and in establishing a boardroom culture that can foster the type of meaningful dialogue between the investment adviser and the independent directors that is critical for healthy fund governance; (ii) play an important role in providing a check upon the investment adviser and providing leadership; and (iii) best fulfill these responsibilities when his loyalty is not divided between the mutual fund and its investment adviser.

D. Other Requirements

The Corporate Governance Amendments require: (i) the board of directors of the mutual fund to evaluate the performance of the board and its committees at least annually; (ii) the independent directors to meet at least once quarterly in a separate session; and (iii) the independent directors be authorized to hire employees and to retain advisers and experts necessary to carry out their duties. The Commission asserts that: (a) the annual self-assessment is intended to strengthen directors' understanding of their role and foster better communications and greater cohesiveness while identifying potential weaknesses and deficiencies; (b) the separate session will give independent directors the opportunity for a frank and candid discussion among themselves; and (iii) the ability to hire employees and others will help independent directors to deal with matters beyond their expertise.

IV. Criticisms of the Corporate Governance Amendments

A. The SEC Does Not Have the Statutory Authority to Adopt the Corporate Governance Amendments and Usurped the Proper Legislative Role of Congress

From 1940 through 1992, the Commission showed appropriate and commendable deference to Congress when it perceived that there were fundamental problems in the mutual fund industry that needed correcting. The 1970 Amendments Act was preceded by an important study conducted by the SEC staff, and the 1970 and the 1975 Amendments Acts were each preceded by four years of lengthy hearings. As it relates to corporate governance, the Protecting Investors report is of a piece with that precedent. It is the 2001 Amendments where the Commission first strayed into inappropriate activity. But by requiring that all mutual funds have at least a majority of independent directors on their boards and that the independent directors nominate and select the new independent directors, the 2001 Amendments were at least borrowing from the requirements of Rule 12b-1 which had been in place for over 20 years.

In contrast, the Corporate Governance Amendments are cut from whole cloth, except to the limited extent that Section 15(f) has a super-majority independence requirement for three years in the unusual situation where the investment adviser has assigned its contract to a third party. Historically, Congress has not differentiated between those directors who are interested and those who are independent for purposes of Sections 15(c) and 36(a), and has seen fit to impose unusual requirements regarding voting by independent directors or the number of independent directors who must serve on a board only where the issue was related to approval of the investment adviser's contract. The requirement in Rule 12b-1 that a majority of the board of directors be independent can be rationalized and justified on the ground that approval of a Rule 12b-1 Plan would allow the investment adviser to avoid spending its own assets, the opposite side of the coin from approving its investment advisory contract. The Corporate Governance Amendments go well beyond that precedent by imposing those requirements on a mutual fund's routine business affairs, not just variations of the conflict of interest with the investment adviser's contract. Whether the Corporate Governance Amendments were supported by the comment letters or were a "good idea" or "best practices" is beside the point: such a significant change should have been submitted by the Commission to Congress with the recommendation that Congress amend Section 10(a) of the Investment Company Act to provide that 75% of the members of a mutual fund's board of directors be independent for all purposes and under all circumstances.

Congress was very respectful of state law when it passed and subsequently amended the Investment Company Act. Corporations that are listed on the stock exchanges voluntarily submit to various corporate governance practices that go well beyond the minimum requirements of state corporate law, and entities like the New York Stock Exchange ("NYSE") laud the high corporate governance standards that companies whose shares are traded on the NYSE must adhere to as an inducement to attract investors from around the world. However desirable those corporate governance requirements may be, they are imposed by a self-regulatory organization and accepted by a company as one of the costs to be borne in exchange for ready access to the capital markets. The requirements in the Corporate Governance Amendments that the chairman of the mutual fund's board be an independent director, that the independent directors meet separately at least annually, that the mutual fund's directors conduct an annual self-assessment, and that the independent directors have access to experts may also be a "good idea" or "best practices," but they are in the first instance matters for corporate law in the state where the mutual fund is organized. The fact that the Corporate Governance Amendments were adopted as amendments to ten existing exemptive rules that have nothing to do with corporate governance is mute witness to the Commission's lack of statutory authority to adopt them -- they are not even an interpretation of an existing set of corporate governance requirements already extant in the Investment Company Act. And it is no less anomalous that statutory authority intended to give the Commission the ability to <u>relax</u> statutory prohibitions in deserving circumstances has been used to <u>impose</u> additional regulatory requirements not otherwise extant in the statute.

B. <u>The Corporate Governance Amendments Were Not Adequately Justified</u>

It is hornbook law that, in adopting rules, an administrative agency must explain why it is proposing to adopt the rule. In proposing and adopting the Corporate Governance Amendments, the Commission routinely cited the scandals from 2003-2004 as the reason why the Corporate Governance Amendments should be in place. Accordingly, one would have expected to find a one-to-one relationship between the justifications for the Corporate Governance Amendments and the principal features of the scandals in 2003-2004. One feature of the scandals was exploitation of anomalies in mutual fund pricing that caused "stale" prices. Another feature was the willingness of intermediaries -- banks, broker-dealers, and third-party administrators -- to violate the Federal securities laws (including Rule 22c-1) and their contractual commitment to comply with the law in the selling agreement with the mutual fund's distributor. Yet another feature is the offering of preferred partners programs where the method of payment is "revenue-sharing," something that was not illegal in 2003-2004 and is not illegal today when paid by the investment adviser out of its own resources. The Commission made no attempt, however, to provide such one-to-one justifications.

With respect, it is very hard indeed to understand how a mutual fund's board of directors with 75% independent directors, with an independent chair, meeting separately once a year, conducting an annual self-assessment, and having access to experts can bring the necessary skill set, surveillance tools, and adequate time to do due diligence to the task of (i) rooting out a determined late-trader, (ii) understanding the nuances of stock prices in a country facing a natural disaster that has imposed restrictions on repatriating profits, or (iii) anticipating a change in the Commission's position on the payment of brokerage commissions for executing portfolio transaction to a broker-dealer that it is also selling shares of that mutual fund. These tasks are more efficiently performed by trained professionals, like lawyers and accountants on the Commission's staff with unfettered access to a mutual fund's books and records, which is why Congress gave the SEC its authority to inspect mutual funds and its authority to require that certain books and records be kept to facilitate those inspections.

C. <u>The Corporate Governance Amendments Will Be of Questionable Efficacy</u>

The scandals (and the harsh settlements) have surely caused independent directors to become even more conscious of their responsibilities. The fact remains that, for many, serving as an independent director is less than a full-time job largely involving preparing for and attending in-person board meetings and telephone conference calls for which they receive an appropriate level of remuneration. While some independent directors may qualify as an "audit committee financial expert," others bring to the boardroom varying backgrounds in marketing, finance, and business. Very few independent directors have a personal background that would equip them to manage a mutual fund or its investment adviser, transfer agent, fund accountant, custodian, or distributor. Of necessity, independent directors depend upon the investment adviser, the mutual fund's independent public accountants, and their own legal counsel to bring important matters to their attention. The Commission seems intent upon changing the dynamics of board meetings and board discussions, and seems persuaded that changing who (or how many) sit at what seat around the boardroom table will accomplish that goal. Even if one accepts *arguendo* the Commission's assumptions and goal, it strains credulity to believe that adding more independent directors, selecting an independent chair, conducting an annual self-evaluation, convening separate meetings, and/or having access to experts can produce an effective compliance program that is more than a shadowy substitute for and incomplete accessory to the Commission's own robust Office of Compliance Inspections and Examinations and its experienced staff.

V. The Long View

1. Mutual Fund Corporate Governance

The scandals of 2003-2004 are unique in the history of the SEC's administration of the Investment Company Act, but appear to validate the concern that the Commission still has insufficient resources adequately to surveil the securities industry and to catch wrongdoers among those that it is responsible for regulating before serious harm has been done. As a practical matter, the Commission appears to be attempting to enlist mutual fund independent directors into its compliance program, deputizing them with new day-to-day responsibilities. To the extent that the Commission is "outsourcing" its compliance responsibilities to independent directors (and not just to the mutual fund's chief compliance officer), it is asking them to do and be responsible for tasks that they are structurally and personally ill-equipped to perform, individually and collectively. The day-to-day management of the compliance function belongs with the mutual fund's investment adviser: no one knows the "ins-and-outs" of a mutual fund's operations better than the adviser's experienced senior executives.

The Commission dismissed the many thoughtful suggestions that were submitted in comment letters in response to the Corporate Governance Amendments. These suggestions included: the designation of a lead independent director and increased reliance on board committees chaired by independent directors; and disclosure by a mutual fund of whether or not it has an interested or independent director as the chairman of its board of directors. It would have been preferable if the Commission had followed its usual approach of cautious gradualism -- it declared the 2001 Amendments to have been unsuccessful a scant two years after they had first been imposed, hardly a sufficient period of time to determine the results of most scientific experiments. Law is not science, but a better decision might well have been to let the experiment begun with the 2001 Amendments have more time to run its course while strongly encouraging the boards of directors of mutual funds to pursue the alternatives that were rejected by the Commission.

2. The Regulatory Problems Behind the Scandals

The core regulatory problems underlying the scandals of 2003-2004 were abuse of Rule 22c-1, aggravated by "stale" prices in the NAV, and aggressive use of a mutual fund's brokerage transactions to provide an impetus to selling activities by broker-dealers and their registered representatives. With respect to "revenue-sharing," the Commission has now prohibited the use of directed-brokerage and has proposed new rules and rule amendments that would significantly enhance the point-of-sale and confirmation disclosures that would be made by broker-dealers to investors.

The Commission has not yet adopted its proposed amendments to Rule 22c-1. The late-trading that was exposed in 2003-2004 has been, and should continue to be, matters of civil and criminal enforcement with respect to wrongdoers or illegal activities. If every investment adviser or broker-dealer involved in the scandals had been screening for market-timing transactions in compliance with prospectuses and/or had actively discouraged abusive market-timing activities, and if each of the intermediaries providing "batched" net orders to the mutual fund's transfer agent had been in compliance with Rule 22c-1 and their contract with the mutual fund's principal underwriter, there would not have been any need for the Commission to consider proposing a "hard close" at 4:00 pm Eastern Time. There is no serious question that a "hard 4:00 pm close" will be disadvantageous to numerous classes of investors in mutual funds. It is poor public policy to adopt a rule that will disadvantage so many investors. The Commission's ongoing insistence that mutual fund directors "fair value" securities is similarly misguided -- that is a subjective task that will not ever squeeze every last opportunity for arbitrage out of a mutual fund's NAV.

A far better solution to both problems is allowing mutual funds whose investment objective permits them to purchase and hold portfolio securities where a market quotation is not readily obtainable or where the investment adviser harbors any doubts that the prices being obtained are not the prices that would be received if the security were to be sold should be allowed to use the next day's price, *e.g.* Trade Date plus one or T+1. It is one thing to attempt to arbitrage on an over-night basis and another thing entirely to make a bet that will take two days to unfold. To the extent that the Commission believes that it is transcendently important to mutual fund investors to be able read yesterday's closing prices in this morning's *Wall Street Journal* so that trading information is instantly available, it should be noted that every investor whose trade is executed on the NYSE other than at the closing price must get that information from his broker or wait for receipt of her confirmation. It seems a much better public policy to adopt a T+1 trading requirement in Rule 22c-1 and ask all of the mutual fund's shareholders to live with the slightly delayed receipt of information than to impose a "hard 4:00 pm close" to the acute disadvantage of so many.

With respect to redemption fees, the Commission should rest now that it has adopted new Rule 22c-2. It was important to empower a mutual fund to tailor its redemption policy, size of redemption fee, and duration of its "stand-still" period to the circumstances that its board of directors believes that it is facing; however, standardization among mutual funds on any one of those points is, at best, a decidedly ancillary policy or investor protection goal and should be abandoned, at least for the time being. With the full authority of the Commission behind them and the example of the scandals from 2003-2004 so very fresh in their minds, there is every reason to believe that board of directors of a mutual fund can identify and implement redemption fee policies and procedures that will be in that mutual fund's best interests.

3. The Costs Imposed by the Commission's Rulemaking

We have all been told that there is no such thing as a free lunch. The Commission has just engaged in a vigorous period of rulemaking, and continues to engage in numerous "sweeps" and inspections. Much of the cost of the rulemaking, such as the salary for a chief compliance officer and the increased compensation that will inevitably flow from the expanded duties and responsibilities of a board of directors, will be borne directly by mutual fund shareholders. Other costs, such as those associated with the "sweeps" and inspections, are less obvious but just as harmful -- it is the rare mutual fund group that has not been asked to respond to one "sweep" or another, generally on an extremely expedited schedule and with the attendant devotion of scarce resources to accomplish the task. The last two years have imposed an enormous time burden and financial toll on an investment adviser's management, its compliance personnel, independent public accountants, and legal counsel. While the mutual fund industry has borne up stoically under severe pressure from the Commission's extensive rulemakings and expansive "sweeps," it does not take a Nostradamus to predict the result will be further consolidation within the securities industry. And it would be a fearless entrepreneur who would now seek to enter the mutual fund industry and bear the skyrocketing costs of creating and maintaining a vibrant and robust compliance infrastructure without serious prospects for having at least $20-$30 billion in assets under management in very short order.

The Commission is charged by law with assessing the costs and benefits of its rulemaking. Because that is an event-by-event responsibility associated with each individual rulemaking, the Commission now needs to reexamine and reassess what it has wrought cumulatively in the cold light of day and redetermine that the new regulatory framework that will emerge from this experience will support a mutual fund industry that can effectively and efficiently perform its business function for the benefit of its investors in a cost-effective manner. It would be wrong for the crisis of the moment, and the immediate reaction to it, to drive decisions that will, in the long run, not be in the best interests of investors. This surely counsels that the Commission let things have a reasonable opportunity to be digested before any additional costs or requirements are considered or imposed.

VI. Conclusion

For the reasons set forth above, the Commission should suspend the effective date of the Corporate Governance Amendments and seriously reconsider whether there are not better, more effective methods for achieving the compliance goals that it seeks to meet. Similarly, the proposed amendments to Rule 22c-1 should be abandoned. Finally, the Commission should, consistent with its responsibility for administering the Investment Company Act in the best interest of investors, continue its laudable efforts to provide leadership in restoring the confidence of America's investors in the mutual fund industry.

Page 140. After the block quotation and before the Discussion Topics, insert the following:

Prohibition of Fraud by Advisers to Certain Pooled Investment Vehicles
Investment Advisers Act Release No. 2628 (Aug. 3, 2007), 72 Fed. Reg. 44,756 (Aug. 9, 2007)[*]

I. Introduction

On December 13, 2006, we proposed a new rule under the Advisers Act that would prohibit advisers to pooled investment vehicles from defrauding investors or prospective investors in pooled investment vehicles they advise. We proposed the rule in response to the opinion of the Court of Appeals for the District of Columbia Circuit in *Goldstein* v. *SEC*, which created some uncertainty regarding the application of sections 206(1) and 206(2) of the Advisers Act in certain cases where investors in a pool are defrauded by an investment adviser to that pool. In addressing the scope of the exemption from registration in section 203(b)(3) of the Advisers Act and the meaning of "client" as used in that section, the Court of Appeals expressed the view that, for purposes of sections 206(1) and (2) of the Advisers Act, the "client" of an investment adviser managing a pool is the pool itself, not an investor in the pool. As a result, it was unclear whether the Commission could continue to rely on sections 206(1) and (2) of the Advisers Act to bring enforcement actions in certain cases where investors in a pool are defrauded by an investment adviser to that pool.

In its opinion, the Court of Appeals distinguished sections 206(1) and (2) from section 206(4) of the Advisers Act, which is not limited to conduct aimed at clients or prospective clients of investment advisers. Section 206(4) provides us with rulemaking authority to define, and prescribe means reasonably designed to prevent, fraud by advisers. We proposed rule 206(4)-8 under this authority.

We received 45 comment letters in response to our proposal. Most commenters generally supported the proposal. Eighteen endorsed the rule as proposed, noting that the rule would strengthen the antifraud provisions of the Advisers Act or that the rule would clarify the Commission's enforcement authority with respect to advisers. Others, however, urged that we make revisions that would restrict the scope of the rule to more narrowly define the conduct or acts it prohibits. . . .

Today, we are adopting new rule 206(4)-8 as proposed. The rule prohibits advisers from (i) making false or misleading statements to investors or prospective investors in hedge funds and other pooled investment vehicles they advise, or (ii) otherwise defrauding these investors. The rule clarifies that an adviser's duty to refrain from fraudulent conduct under the federal securities laws extends to the relationship with ultimate investors and that the Commission may bring enforcement actions under the Advisers Act against investment advisers who defraud investors or prospective investors in those pooled investment vehicles.

---

[*] Footnotes omitted.

II. Discussion

Rule 206(4)-8 prohibits advisers to pooled investment vehicles from (i) making false or misleading statements to investors or prospective investors in those pools or (ii) otherwise defrauding those investors or prospective investors. We will enforce the rule through civil and administrative enforcement actions against advisers who violate it.

Section 206(4) authorizes the Commission to adopt rules and regulations that "define, and prescribe means reasonably designed to prevent, such acts, practices, and courses of business as are fraudulent, deceptive, or manipulative." In adopting rule 206(4)-8, we intend to employ all of the broad authority that Congress provided us in section 206(4) and direct it at adviser conduct affecting an investor or potential investor in a pooled investment vehicle.

A. Scope of Rule 206(4)-8

Some commenters questioned the scope of the rule, arguing that the Commission should define fraud. We believe that we have done so, only more broadly than some commenters would have us do. As the Proposing Release indicated, our intent is to prohibit all fraud on investors in pools managed by investment advisers. Congress expected that we would use the authority provided by section 206(4) to "promulgate general antifraud rules capable of flexibility." The terms material false statements or omissions and "acts, practices, and courses of business as are fraudulent, deceptive, or manipulative" encompass the well-developed body of law under the antifraud provisions of the federal securities laws. The legal authorities identifying the types of acts, practices, and courses of business that are fraudulent, deceptive, or manipulative under the federal securities laws are numerous, and we believe that the conduct prohibited by rule 206(4)-8 is sufficiently clear and well understood.

1. Investors and Prospective Investors

Rule 206(4)-8 prohibits investment advisers from making false or misleading statements to, or engaging in other fraud on, investors or prospective investors in a pooled investment vehicle they manage. The scope of the rule is modeled on that of sections 206(1) and (2) of the Advisers Act, which make unlawful fraud by advisers against clients or prospective clients. Rule 206(4)-8 prohibits false or misleading statements made, for example, to existing investors in account statements as well as to prospective investors in private placement memoranda, offering circulars, or responses to "requests for proposals," electronic solicitations, and personal meetings arranged through capital introduction services.

Some commenters argued that the rule should not prohibit fraud against prospective investors in a pooled investment vehicle, asserting that such fraud does not actually harm investors until they, in fact, make an investment. We disagree. False or misleading statements and other frauds by advisers are no less objectionable when made in an attempt to draw in new investors than when made to existing investors. For similar policy reasons that we believe led Congress to apply the protections of sections 206(1) and (2) to prospective clients, we have decided to apply those of rule 206(4)-8 to prospective investors. We believe that prohibiting false or misleading statements made to, or other fraud on, any prospective investors is a means reasonably designed to prevent fraud.

2. Unregistered Investment Advisers

Rule 206(4)-8 applies to both registered and unregistered investment advisers. As we noted in the Proposing Release, many of our enforcement cases against advisers to pooled investment vehicles have been brought against advisers that are not registered under the Advisers Act, and we believe it is critical that we continue to be in a position to bring actions against unregistered advisers that manage pools and that defraud investors in those pools. The two commenters that expressed an explicit view on this aspect of the proposal supported our application of the rule to advisers that are not registered with the Commission.

3. Pooled Investment Vehicles

The rule we are adopting today applies to investment advisers with respect to any "pooled investment vehicle" they advise. The rule defines a pooled investment vehicle as any investment company defined in section 3(a) of the Investment Company Act and any privately offered pooled investment vehicle that is excluded from the definition of investment company by reason of either section 3(c)(1) or 3(c)(7) of the Investment Company Act. As a result, the rule applies to advisers to hedge funds, private equity funds, venture capital funds, and other types of privately offered pools that invest in securities, as well as advisers to investment companies that are registered with us.

Several commenters supported applying the protection of the new antifraud rule to investors in all these kinds of pooled investment vehicles, noting, for example, that every investor, not just the wealthy or sophisticated that typically invest in private pools, should be protected from fraud. Some other commenters urged us not to apply the rule to advisers to registered investment companies, arguing that the rule is unnecessary because other provisions of the federal securities laws prohibiting fraud are available to the Commission to address these matters. They expressed concern that application of another antifraud provision with different elements would be burdensome. These commenters claimed that the rule would, for example, make it necessary for advisers to conduct extensive reviews of all communications with clients. But the other antifraud provisions available to us contain different elements because they were not specifically designed to address frauds by investment advisers with respect to investors in pooled investment vehicles. In some cases, the other antifraud provisions may not permit us to proceed against the adviser. As a result, the existing antifraud provisions may not be available to us in all cases. As we discussed above, before the *Goldstein* decision we had brought actions against advisers to mutual funds under sections 206(1) and (2) for defrauding investors in mutual funds. Because, before the *Goldstein* decision, advisers to pooled investment vehicles operated with the understanding that the Advisers Act prohibited the conduct that this rule prohibits, we believe that advisers that are attentive to their traditional compliance responsibilities will not need to alter their business practices or take additional steps and incur new costs as a result of this rule's adoption.

B. Prohibition on False or Misleading Statements

Rule 206(4)-8(a)(1) prohibits any investment adviser to a pooled investment vehicle from making an untrue statement of a material fact to any investor or prospective investor in the pooled investment vehicle, or omitting to state a material fact necessary in order to make the statements made to any investor or prospective investor in the pooled investment vehicle, in the light of the circumstances under which they were made, not misleading.

The provision is very similar to those in many of our antifraud laws and rules that, depending upon the circumstances, may also be applicable to the same investor communications. Sections 206(1) and (2) have imposed similar obligations on advisers since 1940 and, before *Goldstein*, were commonly accepted as imposing similar requirements on communications with investors in a fund. For these reasons, and because the nature of the duty to communicate without false statements is so well developed in current law, we believe that commenters' concerns about the breadth of the prohibition or any chilling effect the new rule might have on investor communications are misplaced. Advisers to pooled investment vehicles attentive to their traditional compliance responsibilities will not need to alter their communications with investors.

Rule 206(4)-8(a)(1) prohibits advisers to pooled investment vehicles from making any materially false or misleading statements to investors in the pool regardless of whether the pool is offering, selling, or redeeming securities. While the new rule differs in this aspect from rule 10b-5 under the Exchange Act, the conduct prohibited is similar. The new rule prohibits, for example, materially false or misleading statements regarding investment strategies the pooled investment vehicle will pursue, the experience and credentials of the adviser (or its associated persons), the risks associated with an investment in the pool, the performance of the pool or other funds advised by the adviser, the valuation of the pool or investor accounts in it, and practices the adviser follows in the operation of its advisory business such as how the adviser allocates investment opportunities.

C. Prohibition of Other Frauds

Rule 206(4)-8(a)(2) makes it a fraudulent, deceptive, or manipulative act, practice, or course of business for any investment adviser to a pooled investment vehicle to "otherwise engage in any act, practice, or course of business that is fraudulent, deceptive, or manipulative with respect to any investor or prospective investor in the pooled investment vehicle." As we noted in the Proposing Release, the wording of this provision is drawn from the first sentence of section 206(4) and is designed to apply more broadly to deceptive conduct that may not involve statements.

Some commenters asserted that section 206(4) provides us authority only to adopt prophylactic rules that explicitly identify conduct that would be fraudulent under the new rule. We believe our authority is broader. We do not believe that the commenters' suggested approach would be consistent with the purposes of the Advisers Act or the protection of investors. That approach would have us adopt the rule prohibiting fraudulent communications but not fraudulent conduct. But, section 206(4) itself specifically authorizes us to adopt rules defining and prescribing "acts, practices and courses of business," (*i.e.*, conduct), and does not explicitly refer to communications, which, nonetheless, represent a form of an act, practice, or course of business. In addition, rule 206(4)-8 as adopted would provide greater protection to investors in pooled investment vehicles.

Alternatively, commenters would have us adopt a rule prohibiting identified known fraudulent conduct or would have us provide detailed commentary describing specific forms of fraudulent conduct that the rule would prohibit. Either approach would fail to prohibit fraudulent conduct we did not identify, and could provide a roadmap for those wishing to engage in fraudulent conduct. This approach would be inconsistent with our historical application of the federal securities laws under which broad prohibitions have been applied against specific harmful activity.

D. Other Matters

We noted in the Proposing Release that, unlike violations of rule 10b-5 under the Exchange Act, the Commission would not need to demonstrate that an adviser violating rule 206(4)-8 acted with scienter. Commenters questioned whether the rule should encompass negligent conduct, arguing that it would "expand the concept of fraud itself beyond its original meaning." We read the language of section 206(4) as not by its terms limited to knowing or deliberate conduct. For example, section 206(4) encompasses "acts, practices, and courses of business as are * * * deceptive," thereby reaching conduct that is negligently deceptive as well as conduct that is recklessly or deliberately deceptive. In addition, the Court of Appeals for the District of Columbia Circuit concluded that "scienter is not required under section 206(4)." We believe use of a negligence standard also is appropriate as a method reasonably designed to prevent fraud. As the Supreme Court noted in *U.S.* v. *O'Hagan*, "[a] prophylactic measure, because its mission is to prevent, typically encompasses more than the core activity prohibited." In *O'Hagan*, the Court held that under section 14(e) "the Commission may prohibit acts, not themselves fraudulent under the common law or § 10(b), if the prohibition is 'reasonably designed to prevent * * * acts and practices [that] are fraudulent.' " Along these lines, the prohibitions in rule 206(4)-8 are reasonably designed to prevent fraud. We believe that, by taking sufficient care to avoid negligent conduct, advisers will be more likely to avoid reckless deception. Since the Commission clearly is authorized to prescribe conduct that goes beyond fraud as a means reasonably designed to prevent fraud, prohibiting deceptive conduct done negligently is a way to accomplish this objective.

Rule 206(4)-8 does not create under the Advisers Act a fiduciary duty to investors or prospective investors in a pooled investment vehicle not otherwise imposed by law. Nor does the rule alter any duty or obligation an adviser has under the Advisers Act, any other federal law or regulation, or any state law or regulation (including state securities laws) to investors in a pooled investment vehicle it advises. The rule, for example, will permit us to bring an enforcement action against an investment adviser that violates a fiduciary duty imposed by other law if the violation of such law or obligation also constitutes an act, practice, or course of business that is fraudulent, deceptive, or manipulative within the meaning of the rule and section 206(4).

Finally, the rule does not create a private right of action.

*   *   *

Concurrence of Commissioner Paul S. Atkins to the Prohibition of Fraud by Advisers to Certain Pooled Investment Vehicles

New Rule 206(4)-8 under the Investment Advisers Act of 1940 ("Advisers Act"), which we adopt today, prohibits advisors from (i) making false or misleading statements to investors or prospective investors in hedge funds and other pooled investment vehicles they advise, or (ii) otherwise defrauding these investors. Although the SEC has other ways to reach fraud by advisors, this new rule will fill in gaps in the coverage of other transaction-based, anti-fraud provisions so that the SEC may pursue advisors of pooled investment vehicles who have defrauded investors and prospective investors in the course of their acting as fund advisors. I support the new rule, but I am writing separately to express my disagreement with the conclusions in the Adopting Release related to the requisite mental state for violation of the rule.

In discussing the mental state required for violation of the rule, the Adopting Release states that "the Commission would not need to demonstrate that an adviser violating rule 206(4)-8 acted with scienter." According to the Adopting Release, therefore, the rule covers negligent conduct as well as intentional conduct. My objections to this interpretation of the rule's scope are twofold. First, I do not believe that a negligence standard is consistent with the Commission's authority under Section 206(4). Second, even if a negligence standard were within our authority, for policy reasons, we should require a finding of scienter as part of establishing a violation under this anti-fraud rule.

The Adopting Release offers several arguments in support of a negligence standard. First, it argues that the language of section 206(4) is not limited to knowing or deliberate conduct. In support of this argument, it cites the decision by the United States Court of Appeals for the District of Columbia Circuit in *SEC* v. *Steadman*. Second, the Adopting Release contends that use of a negligence standard is an appropriate method reasonably designed to prevent fraud. In support of this contention, it cites *U.S.* v. *O'Hagan*. I will discuss each of these in turn.

The language of Section 206(4) does not reach negligent conduct. Section 206(4) makes it unlawful for an advisor "to engage in any act, practice, or course of business which is fraudulent, deceptive, or manipulative" and directs the Commission "by rules and regulations [to] define, and prescribe means reasonably designed to prevent, such acts, practices, and courses of business as are fraudulent, deceptive, or manipulative."

The Adopting Release maintains that, because Section 206(4) "encompasses 'acts, practices, and courses of business as are * * * deceptive,' " it reaches "conduct that is negligently deceptive as well as conduct that is recklessly or deliberately deceptive." As the Supreme Court has said, however, "it is a 'familiar principle of statutory construction that words grouped in a list should be given related meaning.' " Hence, it is inappropriate to base a conclusion that negligent conduct is reached by looking at the term "deceptive" apart from its companion terms.

In the Section 10(b) context, the Supreme Court has accorded special significance to the term "manipulative":

Use of the word "manipulative" is especially significant. It is and was virtually a term of art when used in connection with securities markets. It connotes intentional or willful conduct designed to deceive or defraud investors by controlling or artificially affecting the price of securities. n66

The Adopting Release, however, cites for the contrary conclusion a decision by the United States Court of Appeals for the District of Columbia. Indeed, it is true that in *SEC* v. *Steadman*, the court held that "scienter is not required under section 206(4)." The court reached its conclusion by comparing the language of Section 206(4) to the language of Section 17(a)(3) under the Securities Act of 1933, which makes it unlawful "to engage in any transaction, practice, or course of business which operates or would operate as a fraud or deceit upon the purchaser." The *Steadman* court drew a comparison between Section 17(a)(3)'s "transaction, practice, or course of business" and Section 206(4)'s "act, practice, or course of business." The court, relying on the Supreme Court's decision in *Aaron*, held that, in both cases, the focus was on effect. The Supreme Court in *Aaron*, however, placed considerable weight on the terms "operate" or "would operate," neither of which appears in Section 206(4). In fact, Section 206(4) instead uses the affirmative word "is," which would seem to de-emphasize effect. Further, while Section 17(a)(3) speaks of only "fraud" and "deceit," Section 206(4) also includes "manipulative."

It is also helpful to note that Section 206(4), which was adopted in 1960, was modeled on Section 15(c)(2) under the Securities Exchange Act of 1934. Section 15(c)(2) makes it unlawful for brokers and dealers to effect transactions in or induce the purchase or sale of securities in connection with which they "engage[] in any fraudulent, deceptive, or manipulative act or practices, or make[] any fictitious quotation." Hence, as the legislative history of Section 206(4) noted, Section 206(4) "is comparable to section 15(c)(2)." The *Steadman* opinion did not address the link between Sections 206(4) and 15(c)(2).

Section 14(e) under the Exchange Act, which relates to tender offers, also follows the Section 15(c)(2) pattern. Section 14(e), like Section 206(4), includes both a proscription against "engag[ing] in any fraudulent, deceptive, or manipulative acts or practices" and a directive that the SEC "by rules and regulations define, and prescribe means reasonably designed to prevent such acts and practices as are fraudulent, deceptive, or manipulative." Because of the similarities, it is useful to look at the Supreme Court's interpretation of Section 14(e). In *Schreiber* v. *Burlington Northern,* the Supreme Court relied on *Hochfelder's* interpretation of the term "manipulative" in the Section 10(b) context to interpret that term in the Section 14(e) context. The *Schreiber Court* noted that the addition of the rulemaking authorization to Section 14(e) did not "suggest[] any change in the meaning of manipulative' itself." In *U.S.* v. *O'Hagan,* The Supreme Court again looked at Section 14(e). This time, it considered whether Rule 14e-3(a), which prohibits trading on undisclosed information in connection with a tender offer, exceeds the SEC's authority under Section 14(e) given that the prohibition applies regardless of whether there is a duty to disclose. The Court held that Rule 14e-3(a) was within the SEC's authority under Section 14(e) because Section 14(e) allows the SEC to "prohibit acts, not themselves fraudulent under the common law or § 10(b), if the prohibition is 'reasonably designed to prevent * * * acts and practices [that] are fraudulent.' " The lesson from both of these cases is that the SEC cannot effect a change in the meaning of specific statutory terms under its comparable Section 206(4) rulemaking authority.

The Adopting Release asserts that, under *O'Hagan,* a negligence standard is a means reasonably designed to prevent fraud. As the Adopting Release notes, conduct outside of the bounds of the statutory prohibition can be prohibited by Commission rule under Section 206(4). The rule that we are adopting here, however, differs markedly from the rules at issue in *O'Hagan* and *Steadman.* Both of those rules were narrowly targeted rules that covered clearly-defined behavior. They were designed to prohibit conduct, that, although outside of the "core activity prohibited" by the statute, were designed to "assure the efficacy" of the statute.

Rule 206(4)-8(a)(2), by contrast, is as broad as the statute itself. It essentially repeats the statutory prohibition. It does not logically follow, therefore, that lowering the standard of care would be the type of "means reasonably designed to prevent" within the contemplation of the regulatory mandate within Section 206(4). Lowering the standard of care is instead an attempt to rewrite the statute by assigning new definitions to the words of the statute. A potential unfortunate consequence of the Adopting Release's change in mental state is that it is now arguably contrary to statute and therefore might interfere with the SEC's ability to use the rule effectively. Congress included a rulemaking directive in order to give the SEC the necessary authority to provide clarity in this area about the types of practices covered by the statute's broad prohibition, not to alter the standard of care that Congress selected through the language it used. Imposing a negligence standard is particularly improper given that, as the Adopting Release notes, "Rule 206(4)-8 does not create under the Advisers Act a fiduciary duty to investors and prospective investors in a pooled investment vehicle."

n83 *See Chevron U.S.A. Inc.* v. *Natural Resources Defense Council, Inc.,* 467 U.S. 837, 844 (1984). The Adopting Release states: "Since the Commission is clearly authorized to prescribe [sic] conduct that goes beyond fraud as a means reasonably designed to prevent fraud, prohibiting deceptive conduct done negligently is a way to accomplish this objective." Adopting Release at Section II.D. This does not answer the question, however, of whether "fraudulent, deceptive, or manipulative" conduct can arise from negligent acts.

Finally, from a purely practical perspective, I dispute the regulatory approach underlying the contention that "by taking sufficient care to avoid negligent conduct, advisers will be more likely to avoid reckless deception." By an extension of that same logic, a strict liability standard would evoke even more care by advisors. Even if the SEC is authorized to pick the standard of care that applies broadly to all "fraudulent, deceptive, or manipulative" acts and practices, arbitrarily selecting a higher standard of care "just to be on the safe side" has the potential of misdirecting enforcement and inspection resources and chilling well-intentioned advisors from serving their investors.